Ken Lizotte's book is full of tips and tools every speaker should know, with a dash of humor and authenticity thrown in. As someone who has learned the business of speaking the hard way, this book will save you time and help you focus on what you do best – being you!

> — KATHLEEN BURNS KINGSBURY, Wealth Psychology Expert and Author, *How to Give Financial Advice to Women* and *How to Give Financial Advice to Couples*

The Speaker's Edge will become the 'how to' book on maximizing speaking engagements. Ken has provided unique insights and practical and valuable perspectives evidenced by real life examples for any reader to customize his/her own plan to securing speaking engagements.

> — LAWRENCE SIFF, CEO, Neptune Advisors, LLC, and C Level Community, LLC

As experienced strategic growth advisors who use public speaking as a vehicle for getting our message out, we've seen that the world of speaking keeps changing in pace with the changing business environment. *The Speaker's Edge* by Ken Lizotte is particularly valuable because the main focus of the book is on using both traditional paths and digital paths to get more 'speaking gigs.' Ken not only lets us know what it takes to *find and obtain* speaking engagements now, he gives practical guidance on what it takes to keep doing so into the future. This is a book whose time has come and, in fact, is long overdue!

> — PAMELA S. HARPER, Founding Partner and CEO, Business Advancement Inc. and D. SCOTT HARPER, Ph.D., Senior Partner, Business Advancement Inc. Co-hosts, Growth Igniters Radio with Pam Harper & Scott Harper

A key point in this book that stuck out for me is that you need to know just what you're looking for and then ask for it. By being direct about what you want to speak about, you will land more speaking dates than by being vague. Also, you never really know where one referral for a speaking event will lead you, so the important thing is to just get out and speak.

I've had this very thing happen to me. A few years back, when attending a local networking event, I was asked, "What are you looking for?" I answered that I was looking for professional organizations that provide workshops and similar education to their members. I would be interested in leading such workshops if I could only find them. My new contact next asked if I had ever heard of the IEEE.

"You could speak at the local Boston Chapter," he said. So I followed up, submitted a proposal to this local chapter, and next thing I knew I was conducting a workshop there. This in turn led to other interesting developments, from other organizations. Then I got interviewed by the IEEE publication, then a request to write a guest blog.

Ken says in his book that speaking can lead to writing opportunities as well as more speaking. He is so right about that. Trust me . . . *I know!*

— PAUL HUTCHINSON, Principal, Hutchinson Consulting

Ken Lizotte understands how vitally important an effective speaking engagement can be and his book *The Speaker's Edge* brings it all together with his trademark cogency and humor. I've been speaking for 35 years and I know Ken's insights will make a real impact on my future programs. A must-read for every thoughtful professional who wants to "up their game."

— GERRY SHERMAN, Management Counsel to Financially
Challenged Companies, Pathway Advisors LLC

The Speaker's Edge contains a plethora of great ideas, well organized by topic. Every speaker will learn great tips that have proven successful for other speakers. It is a superb resource for both speakers and for people who need to be speakers to advance their careers!

— NORMAN DAOUST, Information Modeling and System Integration Consultant and Trainer, Daoust Associates

As a Ken Lizotte disciple, I can promise that if you follow his advice and remain focused you'll see results – in the form of more speaking engagements! I especially love the "Speaker Notes" sprinkled throughout the book that share tips and wisdom about becoming a successful speaker. Great to have the quotes too from real-life speakers whose success reinforces all that Ken advises us to do.

But one of the biggest takeaways is: get off your butt and just do it! Securing great speaking opportunities takes effort and energy. If you don't have the energy to go after the engagements, you should question if you have the energy to be an engaging speaker at all! Just do it . . . with the help of this book.

— SHELLEY F. HALL, Principal, Managing Director, Catalytic Management, LLC, Author of *Brick Wall Breakthrough. What The @#$% Do I Do Next. Actions for Exceptional Sales and Service*

the
speaker's
edge

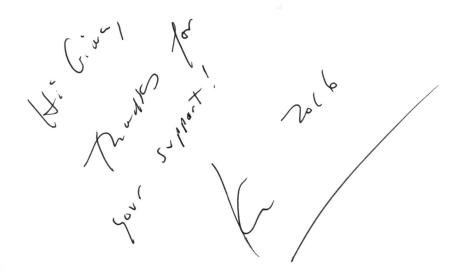

The Ultimate Go-To Guide for Locating
and Landing Lots of Speaking Gigs

the
speaker's
edge

KEN LIZOTTE

MAVEN HOUSE

Published by Maven House Press, 4 Snead Ct., Palmyra, VA 22963; 610.883.7988; www.mavenhousepress.com.

Special discounts on bulk quantities of Maven House Press books are available to corporations, professional associations, and other organizations. For details contact the publisher.

Library of Congress Control Number: 2016934968

Paperback ISBN: 978-1-938548-36-9
ePUB ISBN: 978-1-938548-37-6
ePDF ISBN: 978-1-938548-38-3
Kindle ISBN: 978-1-938548-58-1

Printed in the United States of America.

10 9 8 7 6 5 4 3 2 1

To Chloe, the best of the best

CONTENTS

ACKNOWLEDGEMENTS

PUBLIC SPEAKING REQUIRES AN AUDIENCE, and the hope of most speakers is that each and every particular audience will be as gigantic as possible. What gets forgotten though is that tiny team that helped the speaker make it up onto the podium or platform in the first place.

Writing a book works the same way. That means I would be totally remiss if I failed to begin by properly expressing my gratitude to my own team. Without them, you couldn't be holding this book in your hands or reading it off a screen.

So thanks, Elena Petricone, for masterfully holding down the fort at emerson consulting group while I kept myself hidden away to pound out these pages.

Huge thanks too to my publisher Jim Pennypacker of Maven House Press who put his faith in this book concept and whose resources have brought it to reality.

Thanks as well to Michaela St. Onge and Lauren Fleming, my erstwhile "deputy imaginative officers," who helped me pioneer some of the techniques in this book in their quests to locate and land lots of speaking gigs for our company's client thoughtleaders.

Thanks too to my wife and best friend Barb for supporting me throughout this endeavor. She is by my side, always.

Finally, a rousing Standing-O to the many speakers, event planners, and other speaking pros who generously gave of their time to take my speaking survey or patiently answer my research questions. Without you sharing your experiences and insights, I'd still be wondering how to fill up this book's chapters.

FOREWORD

'VE BEEN A PROFESSIONAL SPEAKER FOR THIRTY YEARS, I've been inducted into the National Speakers Association Hall of Fame, and I've authored *Million Dollar Speaking* among five dozen other books.

I tell you this to let you know I've been around the block a few times. In fact, almost four million air miles around the block.

Speaking is not a "mission." It's a business. It's not about standing ovations and raving "smile sheets" (evaluation sheets), but about behavior change and performance improvement. It's not about pleasing the audience; it's about pleasing the buyer.

Do I have your attention yet?

Great professional athletes love the game, but they also understand that it's a business requiring the skills, discipline, and organization that any successful business entails. Professional entertainers, fundraisers, nonprofit directors, college presidents, and corporate executives appreciate the same fact.

You can speak as an avocation, as a hobby, as a public service. You can join the very effective Toastmasters to hone your skills. But none of that is about running a business, supporting a family, creating a brand. Nor should you listen to any coach or guide or mentor who hasn't had this same epiphany. You don't learn to ski by listening to someone give you advice in the chalet over brandy.

You learn to ski by following a pro down the slopes a few yards ahead of you who's doing what you want to do.

So it's a pleasure for me to advise you to follow Ken Lizotte down the professional speaking black diamond slopes (the green and blue are for the hobbyists). He's uniquely qualified to demonstrate how to traverse the noise and appear unique; how to bend into the turns and negotiate great deals; and how to streamline your attack so that you gain downhill speed in building business.

Moreover, Ken has created options and approaches – equipment – in varied forms to suit varied topics, comfort zones, and taste. His approach is not a "one size fits all," but rather a "try it on and see what's most comfortable." He doesn't insist on regimes but rather suggests alternatives.

He's also a writer and editor, so he can guide you to the maximum impact and leverage of language, both spoken and written. My approach has always been that I'm an expert who happens to speak (and write, consult, coach, and so forth). This book will help you express your inner expertise.

You may be new to the career or a veteran looking for more pizzazz, greater growth, and more challenge. *The Speaker's Edge* will help in all these areas. Ken's combination of rich content and pragmatic techniques coupled with the emphasis on making money reminds me of my first book on this subject, *Money Talks*.

Money does talk, and Ken is a magnificent interpreter.

— ALAN WEISS, PhD, author of *Million Dollar Speaking, Million Dollar Maverick,* and *Million Dollar Consulting*

How Did You Do It?

Too many speakers give up too soon. Like if you're on YouTube, all of a sudden prospects will just start rolling in!

— JIM BOUCHARD, author of *Think Like a Black Belt* and *The Sensei Leader*

PUBLIC SPEAKING IS A LOT LIKE DIETING. When someone has been trying to lose weight and isn't getting anywhere and then suddenly comes upon someone who has obviously managed to visibly shed some pounds, the frustrated dieter can't help but blurt: "How did you do it?" That's really the only question that matters to the frustrated dieter at that moment, especially if a weight-loss battle has so far been a long, if valiant, struggle. "How did you do it?"

If you're a public speaker whose goal, for whatever reason, is to speak to more and more groups, and you've been waging a frustrating struggle in your quest to locate new speaking gigs, you too might be anxiously wondering how other speakers "do it." Whether you're new to public speaking or a veteran who's been at it for many years, how to locate new gigs when they're not easily coming your way will always be occupying your mind, as in:

> "Wow! You got invited to do a speaking gig in Buenos Aires for $10,000 plus expenses? How did you get that?"

Or . . .

> "Wow! You've been hired to conduct a ten-session training series with Magna Bank? How did they find you?"

Or . . .

> "Wow! You're speaking at this year's CEO Summit in Las Vegas? How did you beat all the competition?"

As mysterious and frustrating as losing weight can be, even for those who have done so in the past, landing new, not to mention a lot of, speaking engagements can seem just as mysterious and frustrating, even, at times, utterly hopeless. Though you may know *how* to speak, and you may have schooled yourself in the *business* aspects of public speaking, and you may be a person who views getting up in front of an audience as thrilling, you will nonetheless find yourself from time to time caught up in the throes of wondering where your next gig might be coming from. The well tends to dry up now and then, in fact all too often for some speakers, and such times can make you feel as if landing even one more speaking engagement may never happen. You just can't imagine where to look.

That's why I set out to write about this very subject, and this subject alone. So many books can be found about how to become a great speaker, or about the business nuts and bolts of a speaking practice, or about tools, or about how to dress, or about how to prepare for a talk, and so on. But no books that I know of focus solely on strategies and tactics for *obtaining* speaking engagements. And when you come right down to it, that's really what we speakers think about the most, right? We're obsessed with the answer to the question "How did you do it?"

There's no magic one-size-fits-all formula, however. So if that's what you're looking for here, sorry; close this book right now and see if you can get your money back! There are tested strategies for finding speaking gigs, agreed-upon techniques, innovative tricks of the trade, suggested steps to follow, and caveats, prerequisites, and practical advice from those who have been around the speaking block more than once. Yes, you'll find many of those things in these pages. But quick and easy speaking engagement pixie dust? Nope.

"I honestly believe every tactic for landing speaking engagements works to some degree," says Andy Saks, author of *The Presentation Playbook* (Spark), founder of Spark Presentations, and a seasoned speaking star who has tried, over the years, virtually *everything.* "I believe you could stand on the sidewalk in the center of your town handing out leaflets and eventually you'd trip over someone who has a need for your speaking services and will hire you.

"So the question to me isn't what works and doesn't work – it's which tactics are the most efficient investment of *your* time, energy, and resources. Which will provide the biggest, quickest return in bookings for *you*. That's a slippery question and may differ from speaker to speaker. Something will work for you and something will work for me . . . they just might not be the exact same things."

The mission of this book, *The Speaker's Edge,* is to explore, as much as we can, what works for some and not for others. Until you have tried many or most of these tactics for yourself, you can't come up with a formula that works just for you. And that's what matters.

Andy, for example, has developed customized videos directed toward various potential target audiences so that each audience can see how he would interact with them. This tactic tends to convince a particular event planner in a particular industry or profession or conference venue to hire him. This practice has worked very well for him and, upon first glance, it looks like a best practice that might be one *all* of us should adopt.

Yet Ruby Newell-Legner, CSP, Fan Experience Expert and founder of 7 Star Service, and at this book's first printing the president of the National Speakers Association (NSA), has built an extremely successful speaking practice for herself over 20-some years even though she has yet to produce even one marketing video of her work. And two decades into her speaking success, she has no plans to do so.

"Videos don't work for me," she tells audiences of NSA members. "My customers spread the word about me via word-of-mouth, and so I only rarely get asked for a video. My consulting and speaking occurs over a long period of time with each client, sometimes over a two-year timeframe. I don't think a video would adequately display who I am and how I do what I do, so I have never used one. For my niche market of sports and entertainment, videos are not a key criteria to selecting me as a speaker."

So, as I wrote earlier, this book will explore what works for some speakers and not for others. It will provide a menu from which you can pick and choose what to consider, what to try, what to ignore. This will require experimenting with speaker development methods and tools that may be foreign to you, including ideas you doubt would ever work – if you're willing to be proven wrong! And that can be very exciting, especially when you try an unlikely tactic, really give it a chance, and – lo and behold – what a pleasant surprise: it landed you a gig!

So give yourself permission to play around with unfamiliar concepts, both those you might be skeptical about and those that immediately make sense to you. I want you to customize your speaking development efforts as Andy Saks has done by fashioning your own mix of strategies. What's the plan that's right for *you?* What has conventional wisdom been telling you that *hasn't* been working for you? Let's pave the way to your own magic formula – personalized action steps. While journeying through the pages of this book, your task will be to follow one rule and one rule only: listen to what other speakers have to say and why they say it . . . and then go out and try some of these new techniques for yourself. Only in this way can you learn if other speakers' ideas will work for you.

Ready to start? Then let's turn to Chapter One and examine a checklist of items boiled down from the responses of a cross-section of speakers and event planners I surveyed for this book. Each item has the potential to help you maximize your chances of landing substantially more speaking engagements, just as it has for others. Keep in mind, however, that no one item is *mandatory*. Video Samples, for example, made the list because so many event planners ask for them, or require them, or have told me they're strongly influenced by them. Yet you'll remember that Ruby Newell-Legner said that videos don't work for her, and Ruby is working *all* the time!

So none of the items on my checklist are commandments. Each, however, represents a powerful concept worth considering and possibly adopting. Weigh each item carefully as if it were the key to substantially increasing your speaking dance card. Because it just might be.

CHAPTER ONE

Getting Your Ducks in a Row

First ask yourself: What is the worst that can
happen? Then prepare to accept it.

— DALE CARNEGIE, author of *How to Win
Friends and Influence People*

DO YOU HAVE ALL YOUR SPEAKING DUCKS IN A ROW? Because
without at least some of those essentials you'll be hard-
pressed to succeed at locating and landing lots of speaking engagements, no matter what else you learn from this book.

But before we line up these ducks, let's look at what other speakers and event planners have to say about what's worked for *them*.
Which is not to say that the results of a survey I took on the matter
are carved in stone. Nope, some of these methods might work for
you even if they haven't work for others, and some might *not* work
for you even though they *have* worked for others. But knowing
how the extremes play out may direct you to worthwhile priorities

and time well spent. At the very least, studying the experiences of others can give you a place to begin.

Here's what my speaking engagement survey participants told me about the effectiveness of the most commonly recommended techniques for developing new gigs:

Top Vote Getters

- Referrals and networking
- Publishing

Second-Tier Vote Getters

- Employing a speaker marketing rep
- Internet presence
- Contacting event planners directly
- Social media
- Formal proposals

Few Votes or None at All

- Media interviews (1)
- Advertising (0)
- Cold calls (0)

The most effective techniques clustered around paying attention to relationships and simply getting out there (referrals and networking) as well as publishing your ideas, preferably in a book. While the first is practiced by most of us in one form or another, the second is often ignored.

Yet authoring a book, or even articles published in reputable journals, reigns supreme for a variety of reasons. The credibility that comes your way can be enormous, amplifying your status as an expert and dazzling your potential audiences with the glitter of your name in lights . . . or at least on the cover of your shiny new book. Many in your audience will envy you for your ability not only to get a book published but also to write a book at all. Others will be ecstatic that they can take you home via your book and learn still more about a topic that has now, thanks to your speaking skills, so stimulated their interest.

Certainly not least among reasons to write and publish a book is the fact that many event planners are swayed to offer their speaker slots to authors, for reasons such as those cited above. A majority of my survey-takers have therefore found that publishing ranks at the top of effective techniques for landing speaking engagements.

On the other hand, note the lowest tier results, where few or no votes were cast for media interviews, advertising, or cold calls. Maybe these methods would work for you, but they were reported to be a pure and utter waste of time by most speakers. Though there do exist potential rewards from media interviews, no one had anything good to say about advertising or cold calls.

SPEAKER NOTES

Media interviews can be helpful by providing you with a nice quote to pull out of a published profile, which you can then add to your website or marketing materials. For example: "Keynote speaker John Jones is an exceptional expert on the topography of Mars," said *Science Times.*

Or a published interview might actually lead to an engagement all on its own. This actually happened once to me. I had written a book called *Balancing Work and Family,* and an editor for an obscure, small-circulation office newsletter happened upon it, read it, liked it, and then contacted me to do an interview for the newsletter. I assumed that this would only be good publicity for the book's sales, but I was later surprised to receive a call from an event planner looking for a keynoter for an HR department's weekend retreat. Ya just never know!

The Checklist

So let's get into it. Consider which items make sense for you and which don't. But don't let yourself off the hook, either. If an item seems scary or otherwise formidable, you'd do best to brave your fears and tackle it. The speaking life is not for the faint-hearted.

Motivation

Do you really care about becoming a speaker? Do you feel as though you really *have* to? If you have a fire burning inside you to go out and speak, speak, speak, then no problem here – check this item off your list.

Speaking is a lot like writing a book: some folks really and truly want to do it, and they can't imagine not at least trying to, while others are more ho-hum about it, harboring no special ambition for it. As is true for authoring a book, the more motivated you are to take on the challenge, the more likely you are to overcome it.

But if you don't really want to attain success as a speaker, there are lots of other ways to develop and capture new business. Public speaking, although an effective tactic, is not by any means a necessary one. So decide first if you do genuinely want to become successful as a speaker, and if the answer is yes, read on and learn from this book.

Speaking Topics List

Having made the decision to continue down the path of getting yourself out there on a speaking circuit, you next need to decide what expertise you have to offer. You may of course have multiple areas of expertise and, if you like, you could speak to groups about them all. But you may not want to go that far; you may instead want to narrow down your speaking topics to one or two to take the pressure off. Life is short, after all.

In any event, to be clear about what topics you want to speak about, you need to create a speaking topics list. This consists of maybe five to ten topics, all related to your core expertise(s). Keeping the list down to five to ten helps to not overwhelm both you and your targeted event planners, speakers bureaus, media, etc., all of whom will prefer an easy-to-understand capsule version of your speaking focus. Less is more here, though many speakers make the mistake of thinking otherwise, spilling out 25 or 30 or 50 topics as if quantity trumps quality. Sorry, it doesn't. Topic overload will only cause event planners to throw up their hands in bewilderment and look away. Too many topics, just like too many cooks, spoil the broth.

Your speaking topics list format should consist of a provocative title and a short explanatory blurb for each topic, maybe 500 words maximum. Don't go crazy and write a thesis here!

In terms of titles, keep in mind the wise counsel of Dottie Walters and Lilly Walters, from their fine book *Speak and Grow Rich* (Prentice Hall Press): "Titles are like headlines in newspapers and magazines. You buy the publication because the headline promises information you need or are interested in. . . . The title of your presentations must have this same sense of urgency – make the public or the corporation or association want it *now*." The authors then suggest this format: "HOW TO _____ SO THAT YOU CAN _____," explaining that a title like this points out a problem and then implies that the presentation content will "contain the answers that the audience members can't find, or don't have the time to find." This they call a benefit title.

To illustrate, David Newman, author of the book *Do It! Marketing: 77 Instant-Action Ideas to Boost Sales, Maximize Profits, and Crush Your Competition* (AMACOM Books) and a very busy speaker and trainer, declares "specific topics beat general topics," offering this exercise as proof:

Which is better?

1. Sales Success Secrets . . . or . . . Overcoming the Stall: How to Get Your Prospect Off the Dime

2. Becoming a More Effective CFO . . . or . . . Seven CFO Negotiating Strategies for Vendor Contracts

The correct answers are obvious.

And as for your blurbs, structure them so that they get to the point quickly, ending with a few takeaways. Here are a few of my own blurbs to give you the right idea:

Thoughtleading: The Art of Separating Yourself from the Competitive Pack!
Studies show that positioning yourself as a thoughtleader will result in more speaking gigs, higher speaking fees, repeat business, and a credibility buzz that outshines the competition. Practicing a thoughtleading strategy can make all these a reality! In this session, Ken Lizotte outlines his pillars of thoughtleading as outlined in his book from McGraw-Hill, *The Expert's Edge*. Highlights include: Why you MUST publish a book, best practices for winning speaking engagements (results of Ken's recent book and survey), how to get the media to interview you, and creative techniques for leveraging the Internet.

The 1-2 Punch! Writing & Speaking to Advance Your Consulting Practice

Consultants who write and publish articles and books and who speak regularly at conferences and business events generate a magnetic pull for their expertise that elevates them above their competition. By practicing the 1-2 Punch, you will transform yourself into an *expert with an edge*. 1-2 Punchers cause qualified prospects to seek them out, command the highest fees and most favorable terms and conditions, and accept only the projects they will enjoy. Attend this program to learn:

1. how to publish articles in reputable business publications
2. whether to self-publish your book or seek a publisher
3. how to locate speaking engagements with audiences in your target markets
4. proven tips for writing well and speaking well . . . and closing the sale!

Business vs. Life: Make Them Work Together!

In the midst of chaos, both at work and at home, how can we keep our balance, stay focused, fight off stress, and attain our dreams? Tactics and mindsets exist to support positive outcomes in all such trying areas, which this session will reveal and explain. Attendees will acquire a refreshing approach to life balance and business success that they can take back to their homes and offices and implement immediately. Attendees will also leave the session better prepared to successfully overcome life's curveballs day in and day out, year in and year out, effectively hitting them again and again out of the park.

SPEAKER NOTES

Alan Weiss, CSP, author of *Million Dollar Speaking: The Professional's Guide to Building Your Platform* (McGraw-Hill) and 30 other books, advocates forgoing topics altogether in favor of an emphasis on *value* and *results.* Specified topics, he feels, restrict speakers unduly, boxing them in when what they really should be doing is demonstrating that their work will produce a positive impact on the audience long after they leave the meeting room and return to their work (or home) environments.

He writes, "No company or corporate buyer has ever said, 'Remember Mary Speaker? She received a 9.9 rating. What a great contribution to our business!' But they do tend to say: 'Remember the sales improvements that resulted from Mary Speaker's work? Maybe it's time to get her back in here again.' Focus on your own ego and you might stroked. Focus on the buyer results, and you'll get repeat business."

Carol Bergeron, author of *People Succession: Lessons from Forward Thinking Executives in Middle-Market Companies* (Talent Magnet Series) and founder of Bergeron Associates, says that you need to choose your speaker topics carefully. "I try to make my expertise known so that speaking requests are on that topic," she explains. "I used to speak on a slew of related topics, which admittedly was fun. It was also time consuming and did little to strengthen my brand as a thought leader. Today speaking engagements are focused on a short list of highly interrelated topics, which affords me greater opportunity for creating a rich, valuable, customized experience for each audience."

Target Audience List

Once you've chosen topics for your speaking topics list, your next step is to imagine who would be the best audience to hear them. In other words: who cares? Fortunately someone will, and thus the next item for you to consider will be who those lucky folks might be. Of course, it could happen (take note here) that once you get your speaking topics list out there, surprises could come your way in the form of interested audiences you hadn't expected and, conversely, seemingly perfect, targeted audiences who, despite your expectations, don't really care about your topics at all. But that's what the get-out-into-the-world-and-see-what-happens process is all about. At this stage you try to imagine who your perfect audience match is, then roll your speaking topics list their way and see what happens.

My own target audience list consists of management consultants (at the top of the list) and similar types of consultants such as IT, finance, and HR consultants, and even attorneys. These groups are a great fit for me because they all see the value that ongoing marketing has for *thinking* professionals. In other words, they take naturally to the notion of positioning themselves as thoughtleaders, so they share my view that the two greatest methods for displaying thought leadership are to publish their ideas and then to speak about them to targeted groups. This literally prequalifies them as good prospects for my company's services, because when they come to hear me speak they're meeting me at least halfway in terms of us ultimately forging a potential business arrangement. They are, in effect, a near-perfect match.

Important Question: What business or population segment(s) constitute a near-perfect match for you? Know the answer to this question and you'll have identified whom to put on your target audience list.

Speaker Sheet

Often called by professional speakers a *one-sheet,* this tool predates our current Internet age and thus in some ways held more value in pre-website days than it does now. The concept is that, arranged carefully on just one sheet, all essential information can be presented by a speaker in an easy-to-read format for the convenience of event planners and the like. Ingredients therefore typically include the speaker's name, contact info, photo, and a short bio, a link to the speaking section of the speaker's website, a cover graphic of the speaker's latest book (if any), two or three brief testimonials, especially from event planners who have seen this speaker's work, a brief target audience listing, and, last but not least, a condensed speaking topics list highlighting the speaker's most popular or relevant topics.

In the old days this speaker sheet might have been taken to a printer and cast in stone by printing up a thousand or so copies. Thus it had to appeal to the least common denominator, come what may. However, with the glorious advent of personal computers, we can now customize speaker sheets for multiple audiences and then just spin them out as needed on our own printers or as an attachment to an email responding to an inquiring meeting planner.

On the other hand, some speakers think that a speaker sheet apart from the one resting on their website page is no longer of value, that its time has come and gone. You could even set up multiple web page speaker sheets for multiple audiences, as well as a generic one. That way you could send an event planner a link to the appropriate web page, or you could print the appropriate page out as needed to hand to an event planner during a meeting.

But however you do it, create a speaker sheet – its succinctness could be instrumental in pushing more than one event planner or decision-making committee in your favor when they're casting about for their next keynoter or featured speaker.

Website Geared to Speaking

It amazes me how frequently I see a would-be speaker's new website go up without a mention of their vital credentials or their willingness and availability as a speaker. If they've published a book, for example, or even articles in a reputable journal, a special tab should be set up to guide visitors toward book excerpts, a link to Amazon, a listing of all published articles, etc. All it would take is a "Publications" or "Published Works" section right alongside the usual suspects, such as "About," "Services," and "Contact Us."

And wouldn't it make sense to similarly include "Speaking" or "Speaking Engagement Topics" as a highlighted tab on your menu? This provides event planners with at-their-fingertips access to info about your speaking prowess.

I know you agree with me on this, so now let me suggest the nuts-and-bolts of a "Speaking" section on your website:

1. Obviously your speaking topics list goes first.

2. Your target audience list under the heading "Who would attend this topic?" List audience demographics that make the most sense to you.

3. Your speaker sheet page, perhaps more than one.

4. Video samples of you actually speaking! (More on this later.)

5. Book covers of all your published books, and links to Amazon to permit browsers to learn more and potentially make a purchase.

6. At least five testimonials (but there's no upper limit). Include a photo of the endorser, his or her name, company, or other identification – possibly in a video format.

   WARNING! – do *not* stock your testimonials page with anonymous endorsers, e.g., "Paul G, manufacturing executive" or "L.K., CEO of IT firm," etc. This only leads to suspicion about whether or not these are real people. If your endorsers prefer strict confidentiality, for whatever reason, then it's probably best to use event planners instead or find other attendees who aren't so uptight. Real, live, enthusiastic humans willing to stand up for you and laud your abilities are what you need.

7. Calendar of past and future gigs.

8. Your comprehensive speaker bio and/or your speaker introduction.

Your Intro

Per that last item, your speaker intro, most speakers simply submit their bio for the host or event planner to read and then wait for the signal to jump up on stage. This is fine, of course, a longstanding speaking tradition.

But Fred W. Green, chairman of the CEO Club of Boston, who sponsors twelve or more speakers each year, believes strongly in an alternative approach.

"An introduction should not be just a bio," he insists. "Instead make it the first few words of your presentation, something both eye-opening and attention-getting!" As an example, Fred offers this intro from one of his past speakers:

> So here we are, knee-deep in recession, and who do we bring to speak to you, but a guy who thinks you should be expanding your business. A guy who has helped companies like Jimmy John's, Auntie Anne's, Ace Hardware, and a thousand other companies franchise their businesses.
>
> He has written three books on franchising, one of which we are giving you today as a gift, and a previous one, which he co-authored with the founder of the CEO Clubs, Joe Mancuso.
>
> So, how does franchising apply to the current economic climate? Let's hear what he has to say. I give you chairman and CEO of Francorp, Don Boroian . . .

Lastly, Fred warns that, in addition to emailing your introduction to the event planner, always arrive at the event with a print copy too . . . in case the host forgets to bring this introductory masterpiece!

Video Samples

You should post a few videos that offer a sampling of your work, especially ones with you interacting well with an audience. The first 10 to 20 seconds will be decisive, so make sure to start off with your best stuff. Event planners are as busy as the rest of us, so you need to grab them right away so they'll either keep watching or decide right then and there that you've got the job.

If you like, your video can be much longer – a full presentation of 60 to 90 minutes or a compilation of highlights possibly running to, say, 20 or 30 minutes. The reason for providing more, even as much as a full presentation, is that, should an event planner really, really, really like what she sees, she just might continue watching as if she were sitting in your live audience. If she finds you *that* good, you'll probably get the gig, plus this event planner as an undying, forever fan.

In most situations, however, an event planner will choose you or not choose you based on those first 30 seconds or less. That's because veteran event planners know what they're looking for and thus will make a gut decision lickety-split. Those first few video seconds, then, are *crucial*.

WARNING! Do *not* stage your video with a few friends up front or, heaven forbid, with no one else in the room at all. Avoid a video sample with just a tight shot of you, the speaker, pretending to be speaking to an audience. Event planners can spot this one from miles away, so go for the authentic – your very best moments speaking to one or more bona fide groups, without artificial setup.

Also, make sure that each video sample represents one of your individual topics and not *all* of them. Otherwise, how will an event planner judge that your presentation on topic #3 would be just as expert and smoothly delivered as your presentation on topic #4? Listen to Dottie and Lilly Walters again on this issue: "It does not work to tell a buyer 'I really speak on leadership, but this (video) on time management will give you a sample of my style!'"

If you do this, say the Walters, then event planners will assume "that you are really a time management person who is experimenting with leadership as a new topic" and so they'll reject you! Andy Saks, for example, has produced about a dozen customized videos to accommodate his various topics and target industries: "I would say that having a video helps me get many gigs. It gives them something to look at, a kind of audition."

So demo *all* of your topics on various videos or on a single video "reel." Don't just allude to how great you are speaking on a topic that they can't actually see you deliver.

SPEAKER NOTES

In terms of quality of video, Alex Armstrong, who serves as Jim Bouchard's speaker manager, advises not to go too crazy in the direction of Hollywood-style production values. "Most speakers bureaus don't want to see a highly produced video, they are more interested in seeing something current," she explains. "Even shot with a phone, as opposed to a fancy production with overlays and soundtracks and glitter – many of them actually prefer that!" Instead, she and Jim have focused on substance, developing what she calls short *content videos* that were then made available to their clients and prospects. "It was a big hit," she says, "a real game changer!"

Projector Laptop Adaptor

Which do you use, a MacBook or a laptop PC? Whichever, get hold of the proper adaptor for connecting with a projector supplied by the hotel, conference room, or sponsoring event planner. In most cases you won't need it, but occasionally you will (trust me!), so have this piece of essential equipment with you when you travel. It will occasionally prevent a whole lot of sweating just minutes before you go on!

Wardrobe

The simple message here is to dress your best. What exactly that means for each speaker would take volumes for me to explain and for you to study, and it may possibly require a private assessment by a wardrobe consultant. Thus, in this short segment I can't tell you *specifically* what you should wear. However, I *can* tell you to make every attempt to dress your best, given whatever may be your speaking venue's expectations.

For the CEO Club of Boston, for example, men are asked to wear jackets and ties. On the other hand, at the Arizona chapter of the Institute of Management Consultants, where I once spoke to a morning breakfast audience, men show up with jackets *without* a tie! I wore a tie that day even though my personal sponsor, Bill Katz, CMC, told me the night before that, if I did, I would be the only male in the room wearing one. Guess what? He was so correct!

If you're a woman, I'll leave that decision to your discretion since I'm no expert whatsoever in that regard. Also, women typically aren't as restricted as men in their wardrobe choices. The main thing is, don't violate your own "dress your best" rule. Then you'll be all right.

Speaker Notes

I once hired a male speaker who wore a nice jacket and tie. He spent a few moments giving the audience of job hunters the very advice I mentioned above, but then he inexplicably called attention to his scuffed shoes, saying, "These shoes are not my best dress shoes, and so I would never wear them to an important meeting."

Everyone in the audience had to be wondering, as I was, well then why did you wear them *today?* We weren't important enough? That's *not* the message that you want to send to your audience, unless you never want them to invite you back.

In any case, don't repeat his example! Dress your best, whatever you deem it. Give your audience that much respect.

Book

Great! You have a book (or books) to show your audience or to read from, to sell at the back of the room or to give as a prize for a raffle. Bring enough copies, at least two or three if you're holding a raffle. Don't be a cheapskate! Let your book be seen by folks all around the room, which you'll better accomplish by raffling off more than one.

A raffle is a great idea for collecting your audience's business cards. These are obviously crucial if you're to email them a thank-you note and/or your PowerPoint slides the next day, put them on your contact list, and/or connect with them via social media in order to stay permanently in touch.

Product

This one may take you some time to develop given that much of your product, such as DVDs or CDs, may be based on actual presentations which, presumably, you haven't given yet. Or perhaps it makes sense to wait until you develop your presentation skills so you feel confident that your on-air presence will be the best it can possibly be.

But if you want to ramp up at least *some* product offerings early in the game, take a little advice from speaking guru Darren La-Croix, who outlines how to do exactly that in his free tip video (found on both YouTube and www.darrenlacroix.com) "Get Paid to Speak Tip: How to Start Quickly."

In this video Darren recalls how he got his own speaking practice started by generating two early products, one a book with co-author and already-established speaker Rick Siegel, and the other a set of CD interviews on the topic of humor with already-established comedians and humorous speakers. By beginning this way, Darren not only created product but also acquired a kind of personal mentoring from absorbing his interviewees' lessons learned while traveling down their own roads toward speaking success.

Email & LinkedIn

Does this sound like a "duh"? Yes, perhaps, but while everyone has an email account, some speakers may not have set up a LinkedIn profile yet. And ignore Facebook and Twitter, by the way, unless you personally enjoy them. LinkedIn is what's crucial for business visibility on social media.

As for email itself, yes, if you want to be taken seriously as a speaker and thoughtleader you want your email address to reflect your domain name. So don't use a commonplace email address like gmail.com, yahoo.com, or – gasp – aol.com! Set up an email address based on your domain name.

And if you don't have a domain name? Get one!

Business Cards

Sure you have biz cards, we all do. But do you remember to bring enough of them? And be sure your card advertises you as a speaker. Squeeze it on there somehow, or even arrange the entire card to promote your speaker business. Make sure that people view you in the light that you wish them to see you.

Back-of-the-Room Product

Books, DVDs, CDs . . . enough said. Bring along whatever products you have if the event planner allows you to do so. Be ready, too, with easy-to-read signage that clearly spells out the price of each item along with whom to make out the check to. When it comes to this precious item, leave nothing to chance!

Speaker Manager

Do you have one? You don't absolutely need one, but you might get a lot out of hiring one. We'll discuss this in detail in Chapter Ten.

Excel, Google Docs, ACT, Infusionsoft, SalesForce, etc.

Somehow you must keep track of your speaking gigs. This includes prospects, event planner names, contact info, venues, dates, etc. It doesn't matter what tool you choose to use, just get yourself set up with a tracking system of some kind, then plug in data as it comes in. This will save you a lot of energy and aggravation because you won't have to remember details down the road.

Speakers Bureaus

One seemingly easy way to obtain speaking engagements is to have them come your way from one or more speakers bureaus. Of course, that's their business – securing speaking engagements and passing them on to you after negotiating your fee and travel arrangements. Getting yourself on the roster of a number of bureaus can therefore result in a steady flow of gigs without you so much as lifting a finger.

Sounds like heaven, doesn't it? Except that getting set up with a bureau isn't always easy, nor is it fun and games. For one thing, you'll probably need to have a book of your own that the bureau believes it can sell to qualify as a professional speaker.

Secondly, there's a chicken-and-egg thing going on here too, wherein the speakers of most interest to a speakers bureau will be those who already have well-established careers, to the tune of per-haps 100 or so gigs per year before audiences of a few thousand, and earning speaking fees of, oh, $10,000 per appearance, at the least.

Moreover, a speakers bureau will typically *not* function as a hard-working representative on your behalf, one of their so-called exclusive clients. They will not beat the bushes for you day in and day out. Nope, that creature is something else entirely, namely a personal management firm or a speaker manager or agent.

Speakers bureaus want to earn their 25 to 40 percent commissions (oh yeah!) with a minimum of time and attention spent on coaching and developing you. "We generally field calls or email inquiries from event planners who are seeking a well-known speaker on our list," a rep at a major speakers bureau once told me. "And typically when they hear what that famous speaker's enormous fee is, they'll ask if someone else, with a lower fee, is available. That's when we dip lower into our ranks and offer them an unknown. But that unknown has to also be really good and proven so that our client will be happy, in the end, with this decision to accept an alternative choice."

So if you're relatively unseasoned, but you did make it onto a bureau's roster, the pressure would be on you to do *great* the first time out, and great the second time out too, and the third time out, and *every* time. If you blow it just once you may not get another chance. Also, don't expect a glorious, steady stream of gigs right from the beginning. You may be able to build toward that by being great each chance you're given, but then a bureau may help out with a gig here and there, but that's all.

As to why speakers bureaus can be so demanding, listen to the words of an event planner quoted in Cathleen Fillmore's book *The Six-Figure Speaker:* "Many event planners in fact prefer to work with bureaus due to their extra layer of 'protection,'" Fillmore writes. She quotes one such planner: "With a meeting planner's reputation on the line, [we] can't afford to take any risks. A bad presentation affects the entire conference. So we prefer to work with bureaus, [relying] on their expertise to help us match our clients' needs with the appropriate speakers."

Speaker Infosheet

This item's invaluable storehouse of information about you can save a lot of consternation when the time comes for you to fill out formal proposal forms. So fill the whole thing out as early as possible. By so doing you'll typically be copying and pasting rather than starting from scratch every time you're asked about your topic titles, key learning points, takeaways, testimonials, and so on. This final item is a must!

Please be aware that the information you need for your speaker infosheet is lengthy and somewhat annoying to gather for a reason. The list of information needed has been culled directly from a multitude of speaker proposal forms. It's therefore comprehensive enough to anticipate almost anything you'll be asked. The more complete you make this infosheet now, the less scurrying about and formulating answers from scratch you'll be forced to do later.

So the information you'll need for your speaker infosheet is listed in the following exhibit:

Information for Speaker Infosheet

Your name:

Company name or affiliation:

Title:

Email:

Voice phone:

Cell phone:

Which phone above is your preferred number? (check only one):

   ☐ Voice phone   ☐ Cell phone

Fax:

Snail-mail address:

Website(s):

Book title + publisher + publication date:

Link to your book website or the book section of your regular website:

Link to the Amazon page listing your book:

Your expertise level as a speaker (check only one):

   ☐ Thoughtleader   ☐ Expert   ☐ Medium   ☐ Entry

Number of gigs per year:

Typical size of audiences:

Events to be considered (check all that apply):

☐ Conferences

☐ Company meetings

☐ Organizational or team retreats

☐ Webinars

☐ Regional business

☐ Local business

☐ Nonprofit and pro bono

Your current speaker fees for:

Keynotes:

Breakouts:

Workshops:

Training sessions (half-day):

Training sessions (full-day):

Webinars:

Special traveling requests (if any):

Speaker type or category (check only one):

☐ Motivational   ☐ Technical   ☐ Humor

☐ Instructional   ☐ Facilitator

Other (please specify):

Your personal presentation objectives. List all you can think of:

Will you be available for conference calls if needed?

☐ Yes   ☐ No

Which type of laptop will you be connecting to the sponsor's projector?

☐ MAC   ☐ PC

Will you be the primary contact for questions from the event planner?

☐ Yes   ☐ No

If a representative will be the primary contact, please list name, title, preferred phone number, and email:

Nickname for your badge:

Which industries and/or professions do you prefer to speak to? List all you can think of:

What professional levels do you prefer to speak to? For example, CEOs, HR, business unit managers, CIOs, nonprofit directors, academics, rank and file, etc. List all you can think of:

List any specific companies or nonprofits you would like to speak at (note if any are clients of yours or if you have any contacts within any of these companies):

List any specific professional associations you would like to speak at (note if you are a member of any association listed or if you have any contacts within any of these associations):

List all speakers bureaus that you are affiliated with (if any):

List any meeting planners or trade show reps from past speaking gigs that we should contact. This includes events you have previously spoken at, taken out a sponsorship for, or purchased a trade booth at. Only include those you feel would be worthwhile events for you to return to:

Link to your speaker's video(s) (If you don't have a speaking-to-audience video, link to a *talking head* or solo video of yours (if any) that you feel displays your speaking ability):

List five references and testimonials from event planners and/or audience attendees (if any). Include the following information for each (name, title, organization name, phone, email, testimonial) :

List the five to ten topics pulled from your book that you would most want to speak about:

Provide up to five topic titles and blurbs that you would like to present. Be specific about why each is timely and relevant to your audience:

Describe how your session(s) will actively engage adult learners, i.e., your speaking style, use of group exercises or discussion, props you plan to use, etc.:

Describe how and/or why your sessions are innovative:

Additional or co-presenter name (if any):

Speaker table or podium request:

Desired educational level of your attendees (check only one):

☐ High school   ☐ College   ☐ Grad school   ☐ PhD.

Other prerequisites for attendees (if any):

List five learning objectives (takeaways for attendees), considering the following when writing objectives:

- Describe participant outcomes rather than what will be taught.
- Identify a skill, knowledge area, or ability that may be improved as a result of attending the session.
- Start with an action verb such as *explain, describe, implement, assess, determine, analyze, differentiate, select,* etc.

Write each objective using the following introduction:

At the end of this session, participants should be able to . . .

Your speaker's bio (300+ words, no max):

Your condensed speaker's bio (300 words max):

Your speaker introduction (if different from bio):

Additional comments, questions, or suggestions:

CHAPTER TWO

Focusing on Opportunities, Not Keynotes

Don't wait for a huge platform before you give
your best performance.

> — BERNARD KELVIN CLIVE, author of
> *Rebranding: The Ultimate Guide to
> Personal Branding* (Amazon Digital)

MANY SPEAKERS ASSUME they must be the star of the show if their appearance at an event, especially a conference or other multi-speaker event, is to be worth much. How else can a speaker gain sufficient attention to make worthwhile all the preparation, travel arrangements, time spent both traveling and attending an event, not to mention speaking? And isn't the mere status of being the featured keynoter worth far more than all the less-highlighted breakout sessions or concurrent panels?

The answer is that, sure, in many ways the keynote spot is an enviable place to be. But can other speaking slots offer similar benefits, possibly even *greater* benefits? And can you effectively spread your message and acquire speaker rock star status if you also do your thing in smaller meeting rooms stocked typically with smaller, more-segmented audiences? The answer is yes to both questions.

"Focusing only on keynotes may feel fantastic, but it's also a kind of stupid strategy," says Hugh Culver, CSP, CFP, author of *Give Me a Break: The Art of Making Time Work for You* (Marathon Communications) and a "recovering overachiever" who speaks forty-five times each year. "That's because there are four to six times more speakers needed for 'concurrent speakers' than for just the keynote slots."

To this I would add that a smaller segmented audience may be even more valuable to you than a larger one because here you'll find yourself in front of an audience that is potentially worth a lot of money to you. When a segment is just right for you, its participants will pay attention more closely and often respond more positively and enthusiastically to what you say.

For example, Kevin Dunn, Executive Director of CEO Clubs of America, sometimes offers potential speakers a choice in the matter, explaining to them that if he places them in a keynote position at one of his regular sessions they'll be speaking to a larger audience than if he schedules them to speak at one of his smaller meetings composed of his more "elite" members.

"The large group is fine, but sometimes it doesn't offer the intimacy of a smaller group," he explains. "So the speaker just comes, does her thing, and leaves without getting to know many in her audience in a way that will promote further contact between them. Because of audience size, the relationships are too superficial.

"But if the speaker is a good match for my smaller 'elite' group of CEOs, relationships in that more intimate setting will have a chance to form and grow following the meeting itself. That might lead to mutual business value for both the speaker and the CEOs she has gotten to know in a way that is difficult, though not impossible, to develop out of the larger setting."

So never turn up your nose at invitations to share the stage! This includes serving on (or moderating) a panel or conducting a breakout session, special breakfast presentation, pre-conference session, etc. It could even mean volunteering to introduce another speaker, such as the keynote, or perhaps emceeing or hosting an event. All of these opportunities to get up in front of an audience, even with the spotlight on you for the briefest of times, can lead to the same benefits as the keynote itself, not to mention getting a keynote down the road.

Speaking engagements of any kind are an opportunity to sell yourself beyond that particular gig – they double as an audition, if you will. By introducing yourself to an audience large or small, you give those in the audience the chance to evaluate you, to want to see and hear you again one day, or perhaps to tell a friend or colleague currently looking for a speaker that he or she should hire you. Should an actual event planner be present, you could even receive an immediate invitation to present at an additional venue, and likely one you would not otherwise have known about.

This in fact happened to me in a most unexpected way as a result of my trolling for speaking opportunities one day. I was making warm calls to random contacts. During the course of the afternoon one colleague I called told me about an event planner he knew who was pulling together a national conference in Washington, DC, on workplace diversity, to be held a few months later. Though I wasn't by any means an expert in this area, I did have some experience working with career exploration groups made up of a diversity of participants. Would that qualify? I wondered.

I rang up the planner, Calvin, who picked up his phone on the second ring. We chatted a bit about the conference and about my background, with me rattling off various topics that I could speak on, e.g., motivation, work-life balance, career planning, and Calvin eventually wondered aloud if I might be the solution to a gap he was trying to fill.

"Y'know," he said, "I have expert speakers lined up for nearly all my speaking slots. They represent nearly every perspective: African American, feminist, gay, Hispanic. But you know what I'm missing? A white male! I could use a speaker who could discuss how workplace diversity can be positive for white males."

I could spot an opportunity when I saw one!

"I'm sure I could do that!" I shot back. Not that I was clear at that moment how I could do it. But I was sure I could. So I seized the moment and made a promise to myself that I would try.

"Great!" Calvin exclaimed. "How soon can you get me a proposal?"

Within a couple of days I had whipped up a proposal and sent it off to him. I had skimmed through some books and articles, talked to a couple of experts I knew, and then titled my proposal "Workplace Diversity: What's In It for White Guys?"

I sent it over to Calvin, who responded instantly that he liked it and was putting me on his agenda. He also said that he had no budget for lavish speaker fees or expenses, but he could at least get me enough to purchase a round-trip Amtrak ticket plus a room in the hotel where the conference was being held. I accepted at once because at the very least I'd be getting a free trip to DC, which could be fun, and of course who knew where this topic might lead? He'd essentially be paying me to develop a potential new speaking path.

I set to work boning up further on workplace diversity issues and getting my presentation in order. When the day came I was ready . . . up to a point. I wasn't super-confident since, after all, what did I *really* know about diversity? Other speakers at the conference had been delivering diversity presentations for years, and some even worked on these issues at their day jobs. Thus during most of my presentation I worked at hiding my nervousness and uncertainty about how well I was coming across. I really felt, to some extent, like a fraud.

Finally, mercifully, I got through it and, as well as I could, ended on an up note, thanking everyone for coming. I received courteous applause, and a few attendees came up to tell me personally how much they had enjoyed my talk. This could have been, and probably should have been, the end of the story, except for one couple who came up after I had finished to thank me profusely.

"Great presentation," they said sincerely. "Really enjoyed it." They then informed me that they were involved in planning a similar diversity program that was to take place the very next month at nearby Gallaudet University. "We have the day all lined up," they told me. "We have speakers from every possible perspective. Although there's one type of speaker we still don't have . . . a white male!"

I drew in a breath, hoping this was going where it seemed to be headed. And then it did. "So we were wondering," they asked, "if you would be available to come to speak at our event? I know it's late notice, but your topic today on diversity's value for white males would be perfect."

I mentally checked my calendar while silently noting that there was no way in hell I would say no to this. Yes, yes, I could make it, I replied, trying to seem nonchalant.

Then they gave me the name and contact info of their program director, whom I would have to call to formally arrange things. This gentleman told me he would need a formal proposal to make things official, plus of course my fee and any terms and conditions I required. Since the conference was coming up fast I needed to put all this together ASAP, which I did. And just as quickly the program director responded with a yes. So all of a sudden, whoosh! I was now a bona fide, soon-to-be-professionally-paid speaker on the topic of workplace diversity . . . and would soon have a track record of two major conferences under my belt!

When the big day came I conducted two featured breakout sessions, my expenses were fully paid (airline tickets this time, not train), I was invited to a group dinner with the eight other conference speakers, hosted by the university president the night before at his official residence, and I was ultimately sent a check for the speaker's fee I had requested. My sessions weren't keynotes, of course, but they were stellar enough for a diversity speaker of my admittedly limited stature. Being willing to speak at that previous diversity conference, despite not being offered either the keynote or even much in the way of travel reimbursement, had paid off handsomely within a mere few weeks' time.

Then, one month after that, I was contacted by yet another diversity conference organizer, this one at the University of Florida, who had heard about this "white guy diversity" speaker and decided that, yes, she too could use me. In this case I was brought down to Jacksonville to be . . . you guessed it . . . their keynoter! Again, I received the speaker fee I requested, full travel reimbursement, and, only a few months after I had begun this journey, top billing.

The path to a keynote can thus emanate from a starting point that, at first glance, might seem very far away. But by viewing lesser speaking slots as stepping stones, rather than dismissing them as engagements that are unworthy, you just might get there.

Serving on a Panel

Another non-keynote format you should never reject, assuming the audience fits your needs, is serving on a panel. Panels offer a variety of viewpoints, which audiences appreciate. And, in my experience, that variety often keeps their attention riveted to the overall program in a manner that keynoters sometimes struggle to sustain. While a co-panelist expounds upon an aspect of the panel's topic, you can be formulating in your head what you might add to those comments. That's the sort of stuff that keeps a program vibrant.

Audience members will sort out whom they like best and which panelist seems to be speaking precisely to *them*. The results of this selection process will be different for each attendee, a marvelous winnowing-out process that can save you, the panelist, from wasting your time after the program chatting with people not all that interested in what you've said. Instead, attendees will gravitate to panelists who resonated with them or who fielded a question of theirs during the Q&A session. These are your budding fans.

And such winnowing-out can frequently result in serious new business for the panelist, speaking or otherwise, just as much as if he or she had been a keynoter. I actually got my own current business, emerson consulting group, inc., off the ground with the help of this dynamic. My dream had been to offer my writing and publishing know-how to management consultants for a healthy fee, but at the time I was asked to participate on a panel sponsored by the New England chapter of the Institute of Management Consultants USA (IMCNE). I had yet to land even one client.

The program was called "Writing and Speaking to Advance Your Consulting Practice," which for me was a perfect fit. I had in my twenties been a freelance writer of both articles and books, a practice that had schooled me thoroughly in the arts of not only how to write well but how to see to it that my articles and books were placed with a magazine editor or publisher and ultimately published. This panel would be attended by management consultants whose goal was to publish their business ideas as articles in business or industry publications or perhaps as their first published book. Since many of them knew next to nothing (or nothing!) about how to attain either goal, my participation in this panel would be an opportunity to share with them what I knew.

Also, I wanted to become better known as a speaker, because I knew speaking was a powerful marketing tool for getting known in your area of expertise. Fortunately I had learned a lot about speaking over ten years as a career development trainer, during which I had had many, many speaking engagements that had helped me build up that business. So I could speak to the matter of speaking as a formidable business development skill to the consultants in the audience.

The outcome? Because I took part in a decidedly enthusiastic manner, i.e., I was literally having a lot of fun out there, especially when sharing my knowledge of publishing books and articles, two consultants approached me individually during the dinner hour to say, "Y'know Ken, I've been wanting to write and publish an article for some time, but I don't know where to start. Would you consider working with me?" One week later, after meeting with each and quoting them a fee, both had signed on with me as paying customers in my new career adventure.

Amazing as this was, things got even better two weeks later when I received a phone call from a third consultant, Jim Masciarelli, about "a book I've been working on." He too had attended the panel and had been thinking about it ever since, so he finally decided to call me and say, "I've gotten it as far as I can go with it. I'm feeling really stuck. So I thought maybe you could help me." He became what I call my first "book client."

Three clients from an audience of only 35 or 40 thus launched my new publishing consulting business. Now that might be enough of a speaker success story for you but . . . there's more! Over the course of the next few months at least three more consultants who had attended that panel came my way. Invitations to speak at other IMC events also followed, including featured slots at IMC's national conferences. All this even though I hadn't been the keynote speaker, I had been a "mere" panelist.

Big things happened as a result, big, life-changing things. My experience demonstrates the power of sharing a stage and not getting overly hung up about the keynote slot. As Hugh Culver might put it, find a way to target yourself off the main keynote stage.

Breakouts

Breakouts too can be powerful. Breakouts are those smaller seminars or workshops that fill up a conference agenda, often competing with other breakouts, and for that reason they're sometimes called concurrent sessions. But they'll mainly attract only those interested precisely in what you're "selling," thus segmenting your small-sized audience into a kind of affinity group that's eager to hear what you have to say. So don't turn your nose up at breakouts, either.

While the keynoter commands all the attention at a conference for an hour or so, like a glass of fine wine at dinner, the breakout sessions truly constitute the meat and potatoes of the conference. Though your audience numbers will be less, they'll be qualified, representing those who have a penchant for your topic – one could go so far as to say craving knowledge about your topic and passionate to learn as much as they can. So your overall audience numbers may be smaller, but in terms of genuine interest your audience could be viewed as larger than that of the keynoter, in that its intensity will be higher.

Plus, as a breakout speaker you typically reap a similar level of publicity as the keynoter in that you too will appear prominently on the conference website and printed brochure. You'll be a star in the eyes of those who are familiarizing themselves with all that the conference has to offer, and you'll be doubly a star to those who decide to attend your particular session. Once the doors are closed in your meeting room, and you've launched your presentation, no other speaker, keynoter or otherwise, exists to your excited new breakout followers.

Moderating a Panel

Another role to play that at first glance may not seem like much of a speaking gig is to volunteer to serve as moderator of a panel. Maybe you're thinking, "Oh no, that's no good. The moderator is only the maestro and doesn't get to inject any opinions or knowledgeable expertise or advice." On that score, my friend, you would be . . . wrong! Whether or not a moderator actually takes part in the panel's discussion depends entirely upon the moderator's view of his or her role.

A few years ago it occurred to me that an annual event in my town of Concord, Massachusetts, was missing a key ingredient. This very popular, prestigious event is called the Concord Festival of Authors, which, at this writing, has just wrapped up its 23rd year. It offers the public an extraordinary, three-week, *totally free* conference in which published authors from all genres – mystery, fiction, history, politics, business, science, sports, etc. – are invited to come and give a talk on their book in the evening or on a Saturday or Sunday afternoon at the library, bookstore, church, or synagogue meeting space and share with attendees both the content of the book itself and perhaps also the trials and tribulations of writing it.

One day it struck me that there must be a great many attendees who themselves dream of one day becoming a published author and perhaps finding themselves up on one of these very stages at a future Festival of Authors. But the vexing question for so many of them would be if only, if only . . . *if only I knew how to make it from here to there.*

So one day during a chance meeting with Rob Mitchell, the festival's founder and still its yearly conference organizer, at the local post office – a locale, by the way, where we had chance-met many times before! – I proposed "What if I organized and moderated a how-to panel on the subject of getting your own book published?" This would turn out to be the only such how-to panel ever offered by the festival, but, Rob agreed, it would be a valuable addition to the festivities nonetheless. So Rob responded right there in the post office lobby, "Hey, let's do it!"

It's six years later and that panel has been, and continues to be, an annual event. I vary the actual title and focus a bit every year to keep the umbrella topic fresh and thus encourage attendees to come back. Over the years panels have been titled: "How to Get Your First Book Published," "How to Write and Publish a Book," and "How to Publish and Promote a Book." I also invite four new authors each year to be panelists, partially as another device to keep the panel energy fresh but also to give as many authors as possible the opportunity to participate in this exciting annual tradition.

As moderator I've built myself into the program as a fifth panelist. When I introduce the evening's topic, for example, and set the ground rules, I also offer my own take on the topic, sharing for a few minutes my own thoughts about how to successfully publish a book and suggestions for writing or promoting it, whatever the program's focus allows. I also make myself available for questions during the Q&A session, and as moderator I give myself permission to throw my own comments in at any time. This allows me to be the panel's primary participant as opposed to its quietest participant. I don't hog the microphone, of course, or talk over the other panelists, but I do interject my own thoughts and reactions when I can so that I too am seen as one of the evening's experts.

When you actually organize a panel, as I do this one, or even when you agree to be "merely" its moderator, you buy yourself a ton of leeway in terms of establishing a format that allows you to be as visible throughout as the main panelists. This casts you in a center spotlight . . . just like a conference keynoter!

Remote Formats

In addition to breakouts and panels, consider also webinars, podcasts, teleseminars, Skype events, and others forms of what we might call *remote formats*. All of these can also lead subsequently to traditional speaking engagements, training sessions, panels, consulting, coaching . . . keynotes! You have to be seen and heard, after all, and remote formats, thanks to ever-developing technologies, can enable you to do so.

On the flip side, business coach and thoughtleader Suzanne Bates and other top speakers also view remote formats as great follow-ups to traditional speaking. "Doing a great job on stage at conferences," she says, "will get you additional opportunities such as invitations to do webinars."

An author of four books published by McGraw-Hill, including her first, the best-seller *Speak Like a CEO: Secrets for Commanding Attention and Getting Results,* and her current one, *All the Leader You Can Be,* and a frequent keynoter at major business conferences, Suzanne believes that all forms of speaking formats offer value for the speaker as well as the audience as a kind of holistic approach to landing great gigs again and again.

The webinar, for example, that she says you might obtain as a result of that "great job on stage" will in turn "lead to additional speeches or work." So the cycle brings you around to your original starting and desired ending point, speaking in person at a conference or other event. One hand washes the other, we might say.

In my own case, I had once delivered webinars on a regular basis, as often as once a month for a while. This helped me develop not only my speaking practice but my emerson consulting group business in a number of ways:

1. Those who attended a webinar of mine often went on to purchase one of my books and/or come to see me speak in person.

2. The mere act of announcing to my e-list subscribers that I would be conducting a webinar on "How to Publish Your First Book" or "How to Publish Articles" enhanced my reputation as an expert as well as a professional speaker by planting that picture in the minds of many of my contacts. Because of this they would invite me to come speak to their group when they needed a speaker on one of my topics, or they would refer me to one of *their* contacts who might suddenly be in need of a speaker like me.

3. Whether in person or remotely, it never hurts to practice your speaking skills, or face the challenge of answering a question you've never been asked before, or struggle to explain clearly a subtopic you've never been very familiar with. Practice may not make perfect . . . but when it comes to speaking, it sure helps you get better!

The Dreaded (and Boring) Elevator Pitch

Along the spectrum of speaking formats, you can't get much farther away from the keynote address than the lowly elevator pitch, where you introduce yourself at an event. These 20 to 30 seconds are typically dreaded and disdained by those in the room as something to quickly stand up and get through . . . then sit down! After all, what value could they have? Listening to the pitches of most folks who spew them out, you can't help but be bored by the mundane, repetitive, and sometimes mumbled "messages" that dominate this sad and loathsome exercise. Not only that, but by the time all the elevator pitches in the room are over, you will have completely forgotten the majority of them. And that might include your own!

Yet even the horrid, worth-forgetting elevator pitch should be considered what it in fact really is: a speaking engagement! Yes, it's perhaps the shortest gig of them all, but nonetheless it represents an opportunity to get in front of a willing (at first, anyway) audience and deliver a mini-speech about a topic you know and care a lot about . . . yourself!

Think about it: here you are in a room filled with 20 or 30 or 40 audience members where you suddenly are gifted an opportunity to speak to them all, and in a format that promotes you and your unique value directly. No need to couch your self-promotion inside a "related topic" or pretend that "this isn't about me." In fact, your audience will be poised to listen to what you have to tell them, tuning right into you as you lift yourself out of your seat . . . if only you will be clear and succinct and intriguing, and perhaps a tad entertaining as well. Should they be the right fit for you, they'll approach you during the break or after the formal program ends. And all because of those scintillating 20 to 30 seconds of speech you gave them! How can you pass this up?

Most folks, of course, fail to see it this way, paying no attention to preparing or crafting what they'll say up there. Instead they stagger their way through a half-hearted pitch, pushing out their name, maybe the name of their company, and a vague, too-quick descriptor of what they do.

"Hi, my name is Mort Dodge, my company is called
The Better Way, and we work with our customers to
help them do better in their businesses."

Huh? Mort, please, lemme get this down: You help your customers "do better in their businesses." Say what? *Exactly* what does that mean? You help them do better *how?* Do you sort out their finance issues? Streamline productivity timelines? Help them be better managers? Sales training? Human resources? Paper supplies? Help . . . them . . . how?

You know I'm not exaggerating here. You've been at too many of these dreadful elevator pitch exercises just like I have. So the question is: how can you do better? How can you transform these sessions into something of real value?

The term *elevator pitch,* by the way, derives from the notion that if you came face-to-face with a stranger in an elevator who asked you what you did, you might only have 20 to 30 seconds at best to describe that before one of you had to get off. So most people just don't bother to try, using the rationalization that you couldn't possibly say much of anything in such a short time.

And yet, if you really were in an elevator with someone who asked you what you did for a living, most of us would at least give it a try. So fortunately, despite what millions of resistant "elevator speakers" believe, there is an answer to this social disease. It's called an impact message and was developed by that first book client of mine, Jim Masciarelli, for the very book he had been working on (and had gotten stuck on), *PowerSkills: Building Top-Level*

Relationships for Bottom-Line Results (Nimbus Press). Jim's formula goes like this, using my own impact message as a model:

> "Hello, my name is Ken Lizotte, I'm with emerson
> consulting group in Concord, Massachusetts, where I
> *make my clients famous!*
>   "I do this by helping them get their ideas published
> as a book or as articles, which positions them as
> thoughtleaders and go-to authorities in their field.
>   "Would you like to gain more recognition in your
> target market as an expert with an edge? If so, see me
> later and let's exchange business cards.
>   "Again: Ken Lizotte, emerson consulting group. I
> make my clients famous!"

I then sit down and take in the murmur that follows among those present who have been impressed or at least intrigued by what I have just said and/or how I said it. Many of these folks will indeed approach me at the break or after the program ends to exchange cards.

Compose Your Own Impact Message!

Follow the format Jim put together and you too can grab your audience's attention and defeat the scourge of the dreaded elevator pitch. You might even steal the spotlight from the keynoter! Here's how to construct one of your own:

> **THE ATTENTION GRABBER:** Hello my name is
> _____ (your name
> and your company name, and perhaps location and/

or website) . . . _____
and I _____ (create catchy value
proposition here. Have fun with it!)

THE EXPLANATION: I do this by _____
(add a specific deliverable or two)

THE RESULT: . . . which thereby results in _____
_____ (plug in specific outcome or
two here)

FINALLY: So if you'd like to gain/get/learn to . . . (or
you can phase it like I do: "Would you like to . . .)
_____ (suggest specific
outcome here), come see me at the break or after the
program so we can exchange business cards.

REPEAT: _____ (name, company name,
perhaps location and/or website, and perhaps repeat
your initial catchy attention grabber)

Try this out a few times and see what happens! If any event planners are expected to be there, craft a version just for them. In my own case, I might replace "I make my clients famous!" with "I turn my audiences into authors!"

If your experience is anything like mine has been, you'll surely meet some folks who now know exactly what you do and will want to follow up with you about it. You may even get a few gigs out of it!

CHAPTER THREE

Authoring a Book

Publish, publish, publish!

> — Dr. André de Waal, MBA , author
> of *What Makes a High Performance*
> *Organization* (Global Professional
> Publishing) and 29 other books

POSITIONING YOURSELF AS A GO-TO LEADER in your field of expertise is a must if you're to become a sought-after speaker. And there's no better way than publishing a book to achieve this. No better way, none whatsoever!

A book is frequently an essential ingredient on your speaking resume, perhaps the most essential. This is because many event planners and program directors refuse to even consider you if you lack this credential. There may be exceptions made from time to time, but the bias is definitely in the direction of the speaker who is a published author.

For example, Fred Green, chairman of the CEO Club of Boston, prefers that the speakers he chooses for his bimonthly programs be authors, if at all possible. "A book shows you have credibility," he explains. "Plus I can understand very quickly what your message and expertise are all about if you have a book for me to review. I can make a better decision whether or not you're the right fit with your book to guide me."

In Fred's case, he does occasionally bring in a speaker who is not an author if he feels that speaker's expertise will be especially relevant to his CEO Club members. In such a case, topic trumps credential. But with an abundance of speaker-authors out there, Fred's available slots for such non-author experts tend to be few and far between.

Another advantage you'll have as an author concerns your competitiveness for the highest-end speaking opportunities, i.e., national conferences and keynotes. A quick scan of any year's crop of keynoters reveals the preponderance of authors as speakers, and this will remain true because of the continued value ascribed to authorship. Without a book on your list of credentials your proposal will frequently be tossed out on the first pass. Though you may be offered a panel or breakout slot, reaching the top position at a top conference would be a pipe dream akin to getting accepted to an Ivy League college without having taken a College Board exam. Ain't gonna happen.

SPEAKER NOTES

Beyond mere authorship, what if your book takes off and becomes a best seller? This of course would up the ante sky-high in your favor. Not only would your topic obviously attract huge numbers of attendees to a conference, but you'd also be a household-name author with a mega-famous book title that would drive up conference attendance as well.

Think Malcolm Gladwell, or Martha Stewart, or business book titles such as *Blue Ocean Strategy, The Art of the Deal,* or *The World is Flat.* Should you manage to pull yourself into this category (and luck will be your steady companion if you do because such a miracle cannot be simply manufactured), event planners will fall all over themselves to get you to speak at their events. Big-bucks speaking fees and perks beyond your wildest dreams would be dropped into your lap.

Would you prefer a liter of chilled champagne waiting for you at the podium? Meet you at the presidential suite!

Keeping the Magic Alive

A book also provides a focal point for building a fan base for spreading the good word about you and your availability as a speaker. Your book makes you known to and admired by even those who may never have heard you speak but are fans of yours anyhow. Such intimate followers might one day find themselves in a position to propose you for a speaking engagement, something they might not have done had they not come across, and perhaps even read, your book.

Likewise, a fan who did see you speak, enjoyed you, learned a lot from you, then left that day with your book in hand, could also be in a position one day of proposing or selecting an accomplished expert to keynote a major event. To this person you would be known as someone worth bringing in and/or referring to a colleague at some other organization who is also involved in searching for a credentialed speaker at *her* planned conference. The mere fact of your book taking up space on someone's shelf possibly year after year keeps reminding your fan of your high-level expertise and speaking prowess. You are thus a speaker expert who can be confidently endorsed as a qualified candidate for a critical speaking slot.

Without a book in your name, however, the likely response to a colleague's request for a speaker suggestion often plays out much differently. "Yes, I once saw a speaker on that very topic and he was really, really good," someone might respond. "He'd be perfect for your conference. If only I could remember his name!" We've all been there, racking our brains to try to remember who that terrific speaker was and where exactly we saw her, to no avail.

So our long-ago, uplifting experience fails to help the speaker responsible for it, a speaker who has fallen into the recesses of our sketchy memories. Who's fault is this? Why, the speaker's, of course! A book would've solved the problem by restoring the memory of the speaker's name via a quick scan of the attendee's bookshelf.

I in fact have had this very experience many times myself, but the most glaring occasion goes back to an American Management Association conference in Atlanta, where I had been invited to deliver two breakout sessions based on an AMA book I had written that year. Near the end of the day, after my sessions were completed, the keynoter took the main stage where his motivational session unfolded – to my pleasant surprise – brilliantly. It was then, and has remained since, probably the most outstanding motivational presentation I have ever seen.

Spellbound, I and the other 750 attendees sat captivated by a personal development approach to life that drew from four major segments of society: entertainment, the military, academia, and sports. Employing video screens on opposite ends of the stage to make his points, and running to and fro across the stage, he kept us engrossed, energized, thrilled, and gleeful as he guided us through his framework, insights, and video examples. This amazing speaker exhibited an engaged and magnetic stage presence that never lagged from beginning to end. It was a truly marvelous performance that left us breathless, intensely stimulated, and begging for more.

When it was over we all raced outside the meeting room, pumped up and raring to follow through with his recommendations and next steps. Reading his book on the subject would of course help with this, as might watching a DVD replay of what he had just done. Essentially we wanted to take him home with us and keep the magic of this day alive and growing.

Once we filed out of the assembly hall, however, there seemed to be no line forming to purchase his book. I looked up and down the main corridors but saw nothing. I wanted to also tell him what a fabulous job he had done and perhaps get his autograph on his book's title page. But sadly, this never happened . . . because his book wasn't for sale at the conference anywhere! I'm sure I wasn't alone in my disappointment. The air was frantic and palpating with the energy he had unleashed in us. Unfortunately, this might be the day it would dissipate as well, what with no tool – no book – to revive it later and keep it glowing.

Obviously this wasn't just a disappointment for me and the other attendees, but a missed opportunity for this terrific speaker as well. And if you're wondering why I haven't mentioned his name, it's because, again, I can't remember it! His lack of a book left me without a way to keep remembering him, so eventually his name, company, and other details faded away. All I can recall is the feelings he unlocked in his audience that unexpected day. This alone, however, even for a successful speaker, is not enough. You've got to have a book.

What Kind of Book Could *You* Write?

So does this mean that I'm telling you to just sit down and start writing? Should you then only stop writing after you've filled a few hundred pages of a Word document? Well, not quite, not so fast. You've got a few decisions to make first. Let's start with the most important one: What will your book be about?

Obviously your book should be centered around what you speak on, or wish to speak on. Maybe the answer to this question is obvious to you, and if so, that probably means you're in good shape, on the right track.

But many would-be authors sometimes fall into the trap of wondering what publishers are looking for vs. what the speaker-author wants to put out on the market to serve their own goals. The good news here is that publishers by and large don't typically know what they're looking for – they just sit at their desks or at their laptops, periodically checking their email for new proposals. Viscerally, in an instant, they will decide if a new book idea is a potential great one or not good at all. They are reactors rather than initiators. Thus the book you *want* to write may be exactly the book one or more publishers will, at the moment they hear from you, insist they've been looking for. "I will know it when I see it" applies here.

What book then makes sense for *you?* Although a special hook will be required to set your ideas apart from similar books already out there, essentially the core of your book should be the same as that of your speaking topics list. Here are some examples:

- If you're a speaker on screenwriting topics, you could write a book about how to craft the ending of a screenplay, instead of an all-encompassing book about screenwriting as a whole. Screenwriting professor and consultant Drew

Yanno used this very hook for *The Third Act: Writing a Great Ending to Your Screenplay,* his first book published originally by Continuum Books.

- Maybe you're a leadership expert with an engineering background. You might find a way to merge science principles with leadership development concepts, a combination you regularly employ while working with your client companies' teams. Ex-engineer John Myrna adopted this hook for his book *The Chemistry of Strategy: Strategic Planning for the Not-Yet-Fortune 500* (Global Professional Publishing).

- Are you an entrepreneur and management expert whose hobby is to climb high mountains on the weekends? Your concept might become *Parallel Peaks: Business Insights While Climbing the World's Highest Mountains* (HRD Press), something John McQuaig concocted.

- Maybe you want to write a book about how to advance a speaking business via proven techniques for landing more and more engagements. This will not be a book about every aspect of improving speaking itself, or the business side of a speaking business. Instead it will focus solely on obtaining more engagements with a title like, hmm, *The Speaker's Edge* (Maven House Press). Now why does this one sound so familiar?

Your book needs to work hand in hand with your speaking topics. In fact, your book's table of contents could potentially double as your speaking topics list, or at least be closely aligned with it. The key is not to worry about what publishers are looking for, just as you wouldn't want to modify your speaking topics list to only address what you think event planners are looking for. If you take the lead on what topics you want to offer, and imagine an alluring hook that will set your book apart, publishers and event planners will both follow.

Which Publishing Option Is Right for You?

Which brings us to the next question: which book publishing option would work best for you? Do you want a traditional publisher to publish your book, or would self-publishing your book make more sense? This significant early decision will dictate what your first step in the book-writing process will be, so consider carefully.

The option that immediately comes to mind to many of us is the most ingrained one, i.e., to land a book contract with a traditional publisher. But before you automatically head down this path, let's examine its pros and cons. Many folks assume, for instance, that having your book published by a traditional publisher offers every possible advantage such as being provided (a) an editor who will work with you on a deep level on your book's content, (b) collaborating with a book promotion team who will pull out all the stops to market, advertise, publicize and sell the book once it's published, and (c) pay you, the author, a significant advance so that you may quit your day job (or at least take a sabbatical!) in order to devote yourself full-time to your research and writing. Unfortunately, for the most part nothing could be further from the truth!

Though publishers wish they could provide this, the economics of the publishing world dictate otherwise. Whatever promotion monies, for example, that a publisher may have on hand are typically reserved for their highest-visibility authors, e.g., famous film stars, top CEOs, political celebrities, and previously best-selling authors. Since 93 percent of the half million or so books published each year fail to sell even 1,000 books in their lifetime, these authors with the highest-profile platforms represent a better likely ROI for a publisher's meager promotion budget than does the typical author with a great book idea but a much more limited network or following.

As a result, your publisher will probably *not* be sending you on a book tour or setting you up for bookstore signings, speaking engagements (!), or radio or TV appearances. Instead, your publisher's decision to offer you a deal in the first place will more likely revolve around a perception that *you* would be able and willing to orchestrate such things on your own. This goes especially for speakers.

A speaker who delivers 50 or 60 or 100 presentations every year, for example, preferably to audiences averaging 500 attendees or more, can easily find a publisher. Because despite the rapid and half-crazed rise of social media and Internet publicity, speaking to audiences still excites publishers more than any other tactic. They believe, rightly, that speaking can generate more excitement than any other medium in that you're promoting your book in a dynamic way with many potential real, live, human readers in the same room with you. You're simultaneously *selling* your book right then and there and sending word-of-mouth advocates, i.e., your new fans, off to their workplaces, neighborhoods, and homes to further spread the word.

And if you also have high-level media contacts of your own that you can call upon to promote your book, so much the better. Or can consulting or other business clients or customers also be tapped for sales? Publishers love this too.

In short, these are the kinds of promotional and selling capabilities that a new author, especially one who speaks a lot, might bring to the table to grab a publisher's attention. Though none of these are mandatory, thinking in this direction will carry you further toward landing a book publisher than if you assume the myth that a publisher will be doing all this for you.

The Case for Seeking a Publisher

But if traditional publishers expect you, the author, to do all the promoting and selling of a book, why would you choose to seek one out? Why not simply self-publish? Here are a few pros to offset the cons mentioned above:

- **Prestige and Credibility:** There's nothing more impressive than being able to answer the question "Who published your book?" with a bona fide response that names a "real" publisher. Though only momentary, such a credibility bump will impress whoever learns about it, causing them to proceed to the next, important step, i.e., seriously considering purchasing (and reading) your book.

- **Publishing Costs:** It's the publisher's job to edit, proofread, design, and print your book. If you self-publish, you need to do all this and pay for it. Costs can typically run between 10 and 20 thousand dollars depending on fees charged by the vendors you hire. When you contract with a publisher, such costs are taken care of.

- **Wide Distribution:** Your book published traditionally will automatically be made available to the book trade via such channels as bookstores, libraries, universities, and Amazon. Although some self-publishing companies can offer this service as well, the traditional publisher will usually be more aggressive and better connected in this regard and thus provide a useful advantage.

- **Marketing Help:** Though it's true that the bulk of a book's promotional activity must be performed by the author, publishers do provide some help in the form of press releases, book catalogs, publisher website displays, sending complimentary review copies to event planners and reviewers (especially to event planners and reviewers unwilling to entertain self-published books), and occasionally partnering with authors on special promotions or advertising.

- **Serial Rights:** Established publishers know how to make your book available to foreign publishers and multi-media companies for a fee in return for granting *serial rights*. This means potential foreign translation editions, an audio book edition, excerpts to be printed in magazines or newspapers, or even your book made into a feature film! The publisher of course shares the revenue with the authors for such serial rights opportunities, but the arrangement is well worth it since publishers know how to make this happen while an author would typically have no clue.

The Case for Self-Publishing

Speakers know that back-of-the-room sales create an add-on income stream to any speaking fees or honoraria earned from speaking engagements. While the typical royalty rate from even the very best publishing deals will range not much higher than 15 to 20 percent, direct profit from a self-published book can easily climb as high as 80 percent and sometimes higher, depending on printing costs. This of course is because you've cut out the middleman, a.k.a. the traditional publisher, because in this option you yourself are the middleman-publisher!

Obviously, however, this is only important if your goal is to become (or if you already are) a full-time professional speaker. If instead your desire to conduct ongoing speaking gigs is to promote your expertise, product, or service, back-of-the-room income may not represent the same priority. In such a case, a traditional publisher's royalty rate will do just fine.

However, other aspects of self-publishing can make this option an attractive alternative to seeking a traditional publisher, including control of concept, final decision on your book's cover and interior design, choice of title and subtitle, chapter content, and, finally, the ability to go back and revise your book anytime you like. In other words, no one can overrule you when you feel strongly about how you want your book to look, feel, and read.

The Case Against Self-Publishing

Even so, it must be admitted that self-publishing still carries a bit of a stigma in the eyes of event planners, book reviewers, libraries, and even some readers. This however derives from too many self-published authors over the years falling down on the demands of the publishing side.

So while there's no magic in being published by a veteran traditional publisher, the self-publishing author must take seriously that working in a vacuum could be fatal (to one's *book*, that is!). Thus an expert team of editor, proofreader, designer, and printer must be assembled. That way the professionalism of a traditional publisher will be part and parcel of the self-publishing process as well. In other words, resist the temptation to go it alone!

As I mentioned previously, this will cost you. Using the age-old method of printing books in lots, as has historically been the only way to go, costs for printing alone might be 10 or 20 thousand dollars depending on your choice of paper, number of pages, color vs. black and white, etc. An administrative assistant may need to be hired as well in order to help the self-published author keep everything – inventory, fulfillment, distribution – straight.

However, with the invention of print-on-demand technology, such exorbitant costs are no longer the only option. POD printing options mean book copies need be produced only as needed: one at a time, 10 at a time, 100 at a time, 500 at a time, and so on. The cost to the author-publisher will usually be a set cost per book, sometimes as low as a few dollars for a book the author has decided to price at, say, $25. So look carefully at both printing options before deciding which way to go.

SPEAKER NOTES

Hugh Culver sees the value of an old-fashioned print book as part of a series of steps. "Some people will move up closer to me one step at a time," he says, "using a step-by-step process something like this: Read my eBook, attend a webinar, buy and read my print book, ask me to come in and work with their company or speak at their event."

So in Hugh's experience, a book is a significant prospect-mover in conjunction with other significant tools. Hugh would probably join me in asserting that, while an eBook is an important and popular vehicle today, this digital format should be in addition to the "old-fashioned," highly credible print format.

SPEAKER NOTES

For a comprehensive breakdown of action steps to take regarding choosing the correct publishing option, see Chapters Seven and Eight of my book *The Expert's Edge: Become the Go-To Authority People Turn to Every Time* (McGraw-Hill).

CHAPTER FOUR

Reminding Your Contacts Who You Are

I don't care what kind of a system it is . . . but you need a system!

— JIM MASCIARELLI, global relationship speaker and author of *PowerSkills*

WHENEVER I SPEAK TO GROUPS on the subject of business or career success, I often ask for a show of hands of those who have set up an e-list, basically a compilation of email addresses of professional contacts of all kinds, and perhaps even personal ones. Usually almost everyone in the room raises a hand.

Next I ask that they keep their hands up if they actually *use* their e-list by sending out at least one e-blast a year for any reason at all, e.g., announcing a new website, offering a holiday greeting, offering a discount off their product or series, and so forth. Most leave their hands up in the air, although not all do. Maybe 10 percent lower their arms (and hands), indicating that they do nothing at all with their e-list.

Then I ask they keep their hands up if they send out e-blasts on at least a quarterly basis. Many more hands go down this time, sometimes as many as 50 percent.

Now things start getting serious. "How about sending out e-blasts once every other month?" I ask. Half of the remaining half go down.

"How about every month? Who sends out e-blasts on a monthly basis?" Again half lower their hands.

"Aha, the most wise and most astute are left!" I joke. Though to be honest, I'm not really joking.

"Anyone send out an e-blast every week? Leave your hands in the air if you send e-blasts weekly." At this point only 5 percent of the entire room is still holding up a hand. The blood circulation in this minority's arms is getting really weak by now!

"You're the best of the best," I crow. "Monthly should be a minimum, but weekly, or every other week, is really good. This is the smartest, most effective way to keep in touch with your contacts so that they don't forget you, or what you do," adding, "and to remind them that you're still doing it!"

I'm pleased with this remaining bunch, but there's one more category that even I don't belong to, and that's the exclusive club that sends out an e-blast every day. Their time has come as I put out the question. Most hands still in the air go down – only one or two out of a hundred (1 to 2 percent, that is) keep their hands up.

"Fantastic," I say. "Your courage and consistency are to be commended. How about a round of applause for these die-hard networkers!"

Building a Followship

If you're not reminding your contacts who you are, what you do, what value you offer, and how they can get in touch with you, you're missing the boat. Email contact remains (check the studies on this) the surest way of getting the word out about your services and reminding them that you're still chugging along, still working, still in business.

If you're going out to speak to an audience, and you're not asking for business cards, or holding a raffle, or arranging for the event planner to get you a list of attendees and their emails, then you're leaving money on the table and opportunity to chance. You're assuming that someone out there will somehow, in some way, get in touch with you in the near future and invite you to speak at their gig or otherwise try to do business with you. Yes, it happens, as evidenced by a few of my own stories. But *counting on it* is a bad idea, placing far too much faith in the good intentions of the average Joe or Jane. As the saying goes, "The road to hell is paved with good intentions." So don't keep wandering down that road.

The other mistake many speakers make is to collect cards or email contact info one way or another, then go back to the offices and do nothing with them. If they really and truly do have a semblance of an e-list, as everyone insists when I ask for that initial show of hands, they nonetheless don't bother to grow it. The cards sit there on their desk or on a shelf and eventually get misplaced or tossed into a box. Truthfully . . . you might as well throw all those cards away! You're only deluding yourself, after all.

Networking without follow-up, and then follow-up to that first follow-up, and then follow-up again, is opportunity unrealized, which runs totally against all common sense. Yet too many speakers and other professionals ignore follow-up. When it comes to any kind of business development, the truth is we all too frequently ignore our business friends in favor of seemingly more desirable prospects or event planners who are in fact nothing but strangers. The assumption that somewhere out there lie all our gold-plated prospects, who will jump at the chance to do business with us *immediately* upon meeting us, is ridiculous if it also leaves no time at all to attend to those we've done business with in the past, or whom we've met in one format or another and have initiated some kind of relationship with.

The truly irrational thing about this behavior is that the same, otherwise-intelligent professionals will read books to help them understand how to be successful in business. And such books will tell them it takes nine or ten times the effort and expense to capture a new customer as to generate repeat business from an already-established one. This speaks to the raw power of relationships, demonstrating that it's better to build on the good will of people you know than to keep struggling to establish the same good will with people you don't know. With the former there's a level of trust established that will often draw them your way to do business with you.

So what I'm advocating here is to think of each business contact you meet as a new or continuing member of your personal *followship,* consisting of not just followers past or present who have hired you or sat in your audience but also identifiable prospective followers who might hire you in the future, or influence an event planner to hire you. Your followship should also include vendors, employees, fellow speakers, and even folks you can't in any fathomable way imagine would or could ever help you, whether now or in the near or far future. Because unless they're a person you just cannot stand . . . ya just never know!

So many of my longest-served clients or highest-level speaking engagements have come from sources that I had no expectation whatsoever would ever be willing or able to help me. Had I not kept in touch with them via my weekly e-blasts, had I chosen to strike them off my e-list, those highly prized business ventures would never have come my way.

One example that comes to mind is a featured workshop that I delivered at a regional trade association's annual convention. This invitation came my way via Tom Lopatosky, a member of the Painting and Decorating Contractors of America's volunteer program committee. Tom had seen me speak to a professional networking group he had been a part of four years earlier. I had put him and his colleagues on my e-list following that session, so that when he found himself being asked if he knew any good speakers for the upcoming convention, Tom remembered me thanks to my continued e-blasts arriving in his e-box four times a month ever since.

A simple email from Tom re-established our personal connection, and after a little back-and-forth, shooting his committee a proposal and working out the details of my fee and travel expenses, the deal was done and I had a new gig.

Another time, Paul Hutchinson, a sales consultant I knew from a consultant networking group, dropped in unexpectedly at my office, greeting me in his usual jovial fashion. "Hello Ken! How are you?" He then moved quickly to the point: "Interested in doing a keynote for the area Chamber of Commerce?"

Though my attendance at this networking group had recently been spotty, I always added anyone I met there to my followship e-list, and Paul was no exception. That also greased the wheels for us to sit down for lunch at one point and then to trade hellos at the post office or on the street, which bolstered our relationship. So when a speaker needed to be chosen for this Chamber's upcoming annual meeting, Paul, a Chamber member, thought to pipe right up and enter my name as a candidate.

"Would you be able to ask Ken if he could do it?" the Chamber director replied. Paul said he could and came over personally to see if I would be available. Since the date was clear I told him I would love to. Keynote in my pocket, without so much as lifting the phone.

Ya just never know.

Using Your Followship

With the image of a followship snuggled firmly in your mind, you'll now be able to devise subtle and even not-so-subtle messages that promote you as a speaker who's always on the lookout for new speaking opportunities. When you have a gig coming up, for example, you can announce it full-bore.

When you have *completed* a gig, you can announce that too, with a little report on what happened, i.e., excerpts of what you said, and even a video link of your talk or a segment of it.

Less dramatically, your followship can be reminded of your speaking services in other ways. Place a box in the margin of your e-blasts with a link to the speaking section of your website. Or craft a speaking reminder as part of an e-blast that's primarily intended to announce your new book or recently published article.

Advertising sales reps remind us that advertising only works if it's constantly repeated, not just two or three times but ten, twenty, a hundred, a thousand times! That's why we see the same TV commercials over and over and over and over, ad infinitum it seems, for furniture stores or cosmetics or department stores, in newspapers and magazines or pop-ups online, for the same miracle product or home tool or high-tech gimmick, no matter how many times you try to X them out. It's all about repetition – advertising must *remind* people again and again about a product or service, even as they tune you out, until that grand day comes when they tune you *in* because they've finally come to a point in their lives when they're ready, for whatever reason, to listen to what you have to say. You've made yourself easily available to them when they're ready for you.

But Won't People Unsubscribe?

Aside from the fact that building a followship takes a little extra effort and time (though not that much once you've got your process in place), the biggest reason people stay away from building and employing a followship e-list is the fear that they'll alienate their contacts and annoy them enough to make them unsubscribe. This, they say, will destroy their relationships with their followers.

Yet the reality is that 99.99 percent of your e-list subscribers will remain on your list even if they don't click open your e-blast every time, or even all that frequently. The good news is that even when a contact doesn't open or read your e-blast, and even though he or she may be continually deleting your e-blasts at once, a positive dynamic has nonetheless taken place: your subscriber contacts have been reminded, just by seeing your email in their e-boxes, that you're still in business and, in case they've forgotten, reminded too what your core service is, especially if your subject line is cleverly enough written. This means that you're still their go-to speaker expert should they ever need someone to speak about your topic. Compare that to all your competitors who never show up in your contact's e-box. Out of sight, out of mind, correct?

Eleanor, a fellow speaker, once put it this way: "I get tons of email like everyone else, so I don't always have time to read yours. But I just delete it, I don't unsubscribe because I'm afraid that, if I do, I'll miss something good in the future!" Should that grand and glorious day ever come when Eleanor actually opens an e-blast of mine, it could very well be because something catches her eye that could help her or someone she knows. Maybe it's a book idea that I can help her develop and get published, or maybe it's a group she knows to be looking for a knowledgeable speaker on writing, publishing, thoughtleading, or a related topic. Eleanor would in all likelihood not remember me, my name, my expertise if I didn't take it upon myself to keep reminding her! So that's why I do!

E-list Etiquette

You can see by now that when I speak of e-lists, I'm not suggesting that you purchase an e-list or borrow someone else's. You really have to build an e-list of your own, culled from your day-to-day meetings, introductions, lunches, networking, and speaking gigs. But given that this is a concept built on trust, take care to follow a few simple rules of e-etiquette so that you show your followership community mutual respect:

1. Tell the new contacts you meet when you're networking or speaking to a group that you'd like to put them on your e-list. You can do this in person or you can send them an email after you meet them. But whichever method you choose, also make them aware that you view this as a two-way street and that you would be OK with them putting you on their e-list and connecting on LinkedIn as well.

2. Assure your new contacts that your e-blasts will offer content of value as opposed to blatant selling and

shameless self-promotion. Thus you'll be sending tips, industry information, an article or blog you've written, a link to a speaking engagement or media appearance, an invitation to register for a webinar, etc. This is content that members of your followship community can actually use to their benefit, not yours. And it will mostly, though not necessarily always, be free.

3. You want your followers to know that you'll always welcome similar content from them, since this arrangement is meant to be a two-way street. And you should mean this too. Upon receiving any follower-sent e-blasts, at least open and skim them, even if you can't or don't want to spend more than a few seconds or minutes on them. At least give your followers the courtesy of taking a quick look, since you're asking the same of them.

4. Inform your newest follower contacts that you don't share your list with other list makers, and then never do so. This might be presumed by your new contacts, but it doesn't hurt to confirm it with them. Again, common courtesy.

Collecting Audience Emails

How can you gather the email addresses of your audience attendees? Typically speakers will step up on stage following their introduction and get going, delivering a bang-up presentation, then waving goodbye and packing up to leave. Wow! This makes a presentation, no matter how terrific, a one-time-only event, just like that fantastic motivational speaker whose name I can no longer recall. Not only do such speakers fail to follow up with collected business cards, they fail to collect any cards at all! Talk about a whoppingly missed opportunity!

Instead, include the collection of business cards as part of your presentation, in any number of ways – by raffling off a book or two, promising to send your PowerPoint slides, or a white paper, or a report, giving them a free pass to your next webinar (the date of which will be announced to your e-list), or even, quite simply, asking outright that cards be passed forward to the podium for the very purpose of putting them on your e-list and connecting via social media so that you can stay in touch.

The all-important point I'm trying to impart here is that you should be aware of how easy it is to forget to collect these cards and then be forced to drag your tail home knowing that you blew it, that you left all those valuable cards on the table. Don't just say, "Give me your card at the end of the session and I'll put you on my e-list." Very few attendees will bother, or remember, or want to ("I get too much as it is!"). Plus they'll want to get out of there as soon as you're done and won't want to push through the mob of three or four that's surrounding you.

So build the collection of business cards into your presentation! You have to do it systematically to keep your followership robust and growing. Otherwise it's a painful ride home remembering what you forgot to do. I've done it myself. It ain't fun.

SPEAKER NOTES

I love it when an event planner puts a networking list together of all the attendees and gives me a copy. Everyone who comes to this event will be getting one too, which puts the notion of two-way relationship-building right up there in full view where it belongs, certifying its importance. This practice eliminates the need for you to ask for everyone's business cards.

Just one caveat: Take a quick look to be sure that everyone's emails are indeed on the list. Occasionally an event planner may feel that that particular info would be too invasive. If that's the case, you're back to Plan A, employing whatever device you've settled upon to ensure that you collect those emails!

Sample Follow-Up Message

Following a speaking gig or networking event, within 48 hours, and *before* you actually plug any new contacts into your e-list, always send attendees or contacts an email. It doesn't have to be long and drawn-out, just a simple message to recognize your new professional relationship and to re-inform those nice folks of your plan to put them on your e-list.

As an added bonus, your follow-up is an opportunity to reinforce your thoughtleading brand, perhaps by sharing one of your published articles. Your new contacts will much appreciate this and may even say so.

Here's an example of what I would say in a follow-up email:

> Hello Business Roundtable Members!
>
> It was great meeting you all yesterday and speaking to you about how business book publishing works in today's changing world. I really enjoyed myself, and hope you did too.
>
> As promised, I am putting you on my e-list and connecting with you via social media so that we can stay in touch. I hope you'll do the same and put me on your lists as well. Please note that my weekly e-blasts contain insights into book publishing and related topics. Should you ever have any questions about any of my content, please don't hesitate to ask, and I promise to respond.
>
> I also wanted to share with you my article, "The Myths of Book Publishing," published in *Business Today Journal.* If you'd like to read it, click here to go to my website, www.thoughtleading.com.
>
> Thanks again for a fun event! Until next we meet, be well!
>
> Best regards,
>
> Ken Lizotte CMC, Chief Imaginative Officer (CIO)
> emerson consulting group inc.
> Box 41, Concord MA 01742
> 978-371-0442 (o), 413-521-0013 (f)
> ken@thoughtleading.com . . . www.thoughtleading.com

Pay attention to the simple yet crucial components of your follow-up:

1. Keep your message informal, even to those in your audience whom you never actually met. With you up on stage, they have met you and that's all that counts.

2. Personalize your email if you had an unusual or particular exchange with someone. The two minutes this takes will prevent any feeling that you're just sending them a form letter and obviously couldn't be bothered to acknowledge the special moment the two of you had.

3. Notice also my line about putting each other on your respective e-lists: "and hope you'll all put me on yours as well." Framing it as a two-way street opens the door to them feeling comfortable about contacting you in the future, and trusting you not to apply strong-arm sales pressure on them if they come your way. You're just networking together as two equals. There, you said it.

4. Notice also that a subtle reminder of my specialty is embedded in the title of my article, and I've included a credibility mini-boost by using the words *recently published*.

5. By including a link to my website, I want to drive the more curious recipients toward the possibility of them learning more about my services. This may in fact nudge them toward becoming a paying client sooner rather than later.

In this one, short-but-sweet boilerplate, then, I've unleashed a multiple business development broadside that doesn't in any way threaten my new contacts. Instead it entices them to stay in touch with me and look to me if they ever have any cravings for what I sell.

E-blast vs. Newsletter

Here's a response I sometimes hear when I ask members of an audience why they do *not* send out regular emails: "Ken, doing a newsletter takes a lot of time. I just can't afford it right now." Many folks let this stop them in their tracks.

So allow me to clarify my definition of an e-blast: It does *not* have to be a full-fledged newsletter, and in fact I would propose that it *not* be.

People are busy today, especially with emails flooding their inboxes every day and so much else to get moving on. So people tend to blaze through their emails multiple times a day, reluctant to stop at any one of them. I hesitate to click on even a video unless I know it's going to run less than a few minutes . . . and less than one minute is best!

Also, as our busy commentator above put it, we typically don't feel that we can afford the time to put a traditional newsletter together, with its originally written articles, tips column, events calendar, cartoon(s), etc. All that takes a lot of time, not to mention a lot of effort. Who really has that to give?!

So keep your e-blasts short. You could, for example, boil down my follow-up letter into an extremely simple e-blast in this way:

> I am pleased to announce my newest article, "The Myths of Book Publishing," recently published in *Business Today Journal*. Click here to read it: www.thoughtleading.com.
>
> Thanks for your interest!
>
> Ken

You can see that this could even be tweeted – it's that brief. But don't just tweet such an e-blast, always send it via email, too. Not everyone is on Twitter, nor does everyone on Twitter check in religiously (I know I don't!). But everybody, and I mean everybody, checks their email at least once or twice a day (more likely 20 to 30 times a day). So you'll cover more ground if you send out e-blasts, even very brief ones, as opposed to solely using social media.

Also, do what I do . . . use them all! Send out your e-blasts to your e-list and forward them too via Twitter, Facebook, LinkedIn, etc. Just don't neglect the flagship of them all, email. Only in this way can you be sure you're truly reaching your followship community.

Is Your Website Promoting Your Speaking?

To organize your website so that it assists your efforts at landing more speaking gigs, make sure it emphasizes what kind of expert you are. This demands that you provide tabs not only for "Speaking

Topics" and "Speaking Calendar" but also for thought-leadership sections your competitors will typically not have, such as:

- "Published Articles"
- "Published Books"
- "Media and News"
- "Surveys and Research"
- "Blog"
- "E-blast Archive"

A sign-up box should also be readily visible on each and every page, or at least on the most visited pages such as "Home," "Contact Us," and, of course, "Speaking Services." You want to make it easy for newcomers to sign up for your e-blasts and therefore become upstanding citizens of your followship community. An archive of your past e-blasts is a must too, the better to bring newbies up to speed and familiarize event planners and prospects with your expertise in a particular topic.

So in your speaking section, highlight your speaking topics list and your target audience list, and include your speaking engagement calendar too: where and when you'll be speaking next, and on what topics. It helps too to leave your past gigs on there as well. This adds to credibility because it shows your track record and gives event planners a chance to browse the organizations you've spoken to before, many of which will impress them.

In terms of upcoming gigs, link calendar listings to your event sponsor's website so that interested contacts can learn more as well as register. Make it easy, in other words, for people to come to see you! Also post your speaker sheet, your sample videos, and your list of glowing testimonials.

If you've reached the speaker pantheon by authoring one or more published books, post your book cover(s) prominently on both your home page and in your speaker section. Post also a link to Amazon.com so that your website visitors can actually purchase your book and see your Amazon readers' testimonials. Again, *make things easy* for those who are showing an interest in you.

CHAPTER FIVE

Driving Event Planners Your Way

Make them come to you!

> — Alan Weiss, PhD, author of *Million Dollar Speaking* (McGraw-Hill)

MAKING YOURSELF FAMOUS is the single best goal you could have as you push along toward speaker success. You may never become mega-famous, but you can definitely elevate your notoriety among your chosen target audience markets, if you use my five pillars of thoughtleading framework (outlined below) when promoting your speaking services. By doing so, you'll begin driving event planners your way.

Anyone, yes *anyone,* can become more famous if they set their minds to it. After all, this is the intent of marketing, advertising, publicity, networking, and all those other standard practices that any expert, company, or speaker must do to keep business flowing. Even a nonprofit or charity must keep revenue coming in if it's to have an impact and keep its doors open. Thus even a nonprofit or charity needs to become as well-known as possible, another way of saying it must make itself famous.

How can my five pillars help with this? Let's take a look.

PILLAR #1
Publishing Your Ideas

I have already insisted that writing and publishing a book is essential for expanding your schedule of speaking engagements. But writing and publishing articles can also help in establishing yourself as a thoughtleading speaker. Though a book will sit on the highest rung, publishing articles in your target audience's publications isn't far below – especially if the article is about the very topic you'll be speaking about. Then you plunk it down on everyone's table setting or chair before you begin. To attain the acceptance of a reputable publication (which could even mean the newsletter or e-zine of the organization that's sponsoring your talk) is an impressive feat to those who have come to hear you speak. Thus articles as well as books have their place in elevating your credibility and making you more famous.

Books and articles together constitute Pillar #1 of my framework, i.e., Publishing Your Ideas. In concert with the other four pillars – speaking to groups, fresh thinking, creative leveraging of the Internet, and vigorous use of traditional media – you can seriously pump up both your visibility and credibility on the road to making yourself better known to audiences and event planners.

How fabulously this can work was brought home to me after I wrote an article for the American Management Association's glossy monthly business journal. At the time I had been delivering what was becoming a popular presentation on how to become more creative in both work and play, and so I decided to pitch the same idea to the AMA editor. She actually liked the idea so much that she called me on the phone! Normally an email response is the best your pitch will generate, even when the editor is excited! But this time she wanted to learn more about what I had in mind, so we chatted a bit. Then she requested a 2,000-word draft aimed at AMA's target readership of mid- to high-level managers and executives. "Would that be possible?" she asked.

"No problem!" I exclaimed. Then I said goodbye, hung up, and went to work. Ultimately my article was accepted and ran a few months later. This allowed me to lay it out in a reprint format with clear attribution – "Published by the American Management Association" – in large, bold type at the top of the page. My reprint could now be used as a high-credibility tool when I went out to do my creativity thing.

A few weeks after publication, however, I got a call out of the blue that turned into an unexpected bonus. An event planner for a major trade conference had seen my article and decided the topic might make a terrific keynote. We discussed my ideas on the subject and why she felt her attendees might benefit from them. Then she asked if I would be interested in speaking at her conference, to be held in Princeton, New Jersey.

"No problem!" I blurted (I was beginning to like this phrase!). Then we worked out such details as speaker fee and travel expenses. After hanging up I sat back a moment, stunned at what had just happened. Merely writing and publishing an article about my speaker topic had attracted a qualified event planner. Who knew?

So publishing articles can work. It can help to spread your name, speaker bio, and topic toward the right people, raise your Google ranking, and offer you fresh content for your e-blasts and social media accounts. Remember to always cite the publication that published your article, bcause this is what distinguishes this category of publishing from your blog or tweets. In this case someone else, presumably a relevant and impressive-sounding target publication, has vetted you and invested in you, so don't leave this minor detail out!

Also, once you do have a book, pull out excerpts from it and craft them into stand-alone articles that you can pitch to editors. You'll now be hitting on all publishing cylinders by getting the word out in both book form and article form, using excerpts to promote not only your speaking services but your book and therefore yourself as well.

SPEAKER NOTES

"Move followers to buyers," advises Hugh Culver. "Content marketing is here to stay and that's a good thing. You have volumes of content, now you need to create a simple system to get that out to the world every week (not when you feel like it). The good news is that the

> discipline of creating consistent content will make you a better speaker."

PILLAR #2
Speaking to Groups and Followers

Obviously I don't need to dwell on this pillar, since you wouldn't be reading this book if you weren't already convinced it was worth doing. So I'll only emphasize a few basic points that tie public speakers to the thoughtleading framework.

In addition to its capacity to offer its practitioners a lucrative and exhilarating career, speaking to groups also provides value in other ways, particularly on a personal level. Four special values come to mind:

1. Prepping for a presentation can deepen and refresh your thoughts and hypotheses.

2. The mere act of delivering a presentation forces you to articulate and defend such thoughts and hypotheses right on the spot. This will tend to deepen them even more!

3. Eliciting audience questions and feedback can sometimes enlighten you in a manner that transforms your own assumptions, sending you off in an entirely new direction.

4. Such new directions can lead to future topics that become the basis for a new book, new articles, and a new speaking topics list.

PILLAR #3

Keeping Your Edge with Fresh Thinking

Each of us faces choices every day that dictate whether or not we'll stay on our current path or switch to a new one. Often our choice is to stay on the same path, perhaps with only minor adjustments, which means relying on what we already know. There's nothing wrong with that, per se.

But true practitioners of thoughtleading also like to periodically think great thoughts. When you do that your ideas evolve, develop, and blossom. Such fresh thinking can enormously benefit your speaking pillar as it pushes you to search out new answers to unexpected questions. By taking surveys and compiling new data, conducting interviews to learn what others think and believe, and generating discussions about topics you haven't explored before, you'll hatch new topics to communicate to others.

So from time to time conduct original research. You'll identify and articulate new conclusions for the good of all.

SPEAKER NOTES

Alex Armstrong and Jim Bouchard say, "You need to become an expert in something. A lot of speakers have way too many products, much too scattered. They claim too much that they can do. That changed for us when we learned how to focus and go after clients we

> identified and then produce products just for *them*. Research for our books is now directed toward new ideas for building leaders. Once we chose *leadership expert* as Jim's focus, the rest of it started falling into place."

PILLAR #4
Creatively Leveraging the Internet

In other sections of this book we've explored the tremendous value of utilizing e-lists to market your speaking skills and services, as well as techniques for organizing your website for the same purposes. In this section I'll discuss examples of creatively leveraging the Internet.

Channels that you can use to get your name out include blogging, Twitter, LinkedIn, Facebook, Tumblr, Instagram, YouTube, Internet news releases, Amazon book promotion services, and numerous other social media options. Forwarding your e-blasts to these channels, as I do, ensures that your messages get out to as wide a following as possible. All of this represents creative leveraging of the Internet.

These relatively new channels exist, so why not use them? Don't, however, forget the supremacy of e-blasts to your e-list! Many of the social media channels have been touted as the latest and greatest way to go by their advocates, despite very little actual data to back up their efficacy. Sure, it can feel like you're doing something by tweeting your momentary thoughts a hundred times a day, but can anyone actually back that up with real results?

Business coach Jim Pouliopoulos puts it this way: "What I've found does not work in terms of obtaining new speaking gigs is to wait for a gig to come my way via social media, or my blog, etc. That never works, in my experience."

Allan Lowe, MBA, a specialist on Construction Team Collaboration, agrees, stating that a "strong Internet presence is the goal to aspire to, with a Google ranking of #1." But not, he adds, social media.

So do find ways to access the Internet, but don't do so blindly, and don't assume that a lot of activity, such as constant tweeting or blogging, will be enough. Develop your e-list as your basic Internet communication channel, then add other social media channels as you wish to augment your e-blasts. That approach has been proven to produce more direct results than merely employing social media channels on their own.

SPEAKER NOTES

Patrick O'Malley, NSA keynote speaker and expert on social networking and Google advertising, says "Your best chance to get and maintain a high Google ranking *quickly,* without spending tens of thousands of dollars, lies in creating YouTube videos."

PILLAR #5

Making Vigorous Use of Traditional Media

All too often when you win media attention, in even a national vehicle such as the *Wall Street Journal, Harvard Business Review,* or CNN, absolutely nothing perceptible happens as a result. Yes, it's true . . . nothing whatsoever!

Plus there's always the chance that you'll be misquoted, your name will be misspelled, your company name will be left out, the title of your book will be mangled, or you'll be left out of the article, despite spending perhaps an hour or more with a reporter!

It's great fun to be interviewed by a member of the press, especially from a highly prestigious publication. And of course even if you don't make the article, you can always add to your speaker introduction that you've been interviewed by *Fortune, Business Week,* and the *New York Times,* as I can, even though (sniff! sniff!) when each resulting article came out, I wasn't quoted in any of them! Still, I was considered expert enough to be interviewed by these uppermost news journals, so I'll take what I can get!

But given these truths, why would anyone bother with the media in the first place? Why not focus instead only on books and articles, delve into fresh thinking from time to time, creatively leverage the Internet, and of course speak, speak, speak to one's target audiences? Why bother with Pillar #5 at all?

It's a good question, for sure, and here's the answer: the Nudge Factor. In combination with the other four pillars, vigorous use of traditional media has the capacity to nudge potential followers your way and thus help you arrive at that all-important tipping point. How often, for example, have you heard about a new book in a variety of ways – a book review, the author interviewed on the radio, a TV commentator who mentions the book, a profile of the author in your morning newspaper – and you say to yourself, "I have to get a copy of this book."

But you may not have cared about the book when you first heard about it. With each succeeding media nudge, however, you learned a little bit more and a little bit more, so that your understanding and interest slowly grew. By the fourth or fifth nudge, you had heard enough. You were moved to actually buy the book and read it!

On the thoughtleader's side of the fence, this is what happens next: "Oh yeah, I've heard about you," someone will say. "You wrote that book on XYZ, right? And you speak at conferences about XYZ too, right?"

You are happy and flattered that this new fan knows about you. So you have to ask how she knows this. How did she hear of you?

"I really don't know," comes the reply. "I've been hearing about you here and there. From all over, really."

This is the Nudge Factor. Vigorous use of traditional media can help.

CHAPTER SIX

Making Formal Proposals

What's a big mistake speakers make? Waiting for a conference planner to come to YOU!

> — LOUISE A. KORVER, Managing Partner,
> Global Executive Development
> Partners LLC and author of *Successful Onboarding* (Executive Development)

I N MANY WAYS the bane of the hunt for speaking engagements is the so-called formal proposal process. This involves filling out fields and boxes on online proposal forms in order to be considered for the more important conferences, especially the national ones that are sponsored by professional associations and companies. The reason I call it a bane is because there's no common application used by all these thousands of conference sponsors in the way that there's now the growing use of a common application form when applying for colleges (high school seniors, be thankful!). Public speakers must resign themselves instead to applications composed by each and every organization that's out there opening up its doors to speaker applicants for its next big event. This ends up creating a myriad of combinations of questions and requirements so that each application becomes a world unto its own. So don't expect to breeze through any one app!

Unless, of course, you're smart enough to prepare yourself! This means working on answers beforehand to the most likely questions you'll encounter. Then you can plug them all into one personal data center, e.g., a Word document, so that copying and pasting is the order of the day as you merrily roll from one online proposal form to the next.

Filling out the speaker infosheet I shared with you back in Chapter One will help you. You'll recall that it contains both common and uncommon questions and requests that I've come across over the years, meaning that I've waged that battle for you. If you've waged your own battles with such formal online proposals, you may even have encountered questions that I haven't, which are therefore missing from my form. If you find this to be the case, please email your own finds to me at ken@thoughtleading.com so that I can add them to the infosheet on my website. My goal is keep my infosheet as comprehensive and up-to-date as possible for the benefit of anyone visiting my site. Thanks in advance for your help.

Winning the formal proposal game is a combination of playing the numbers and luck, so it's just like Vegas! The fact is that even if you have everything going for you – best-selling book, great speaking track record and testimonials, word-of-mouth recommendation from someone on the inside of an organization, a super speaker video, reasonable fees – you still need to pound away at those conference websites, as many as you can stomach, day in and day out, and keep your fingers crossed. This formal proposal game is where the bulk of the competition is, so you'll likely lose out on any number of proposals that you just knew you were perfect for. The problem is that you just can't know what's going on inside that speaker selection team's collective head, or the singular head of the event planner in charge.

Maybe it came down to you and one other speaker, and for whatever reason the other one got the nod. Or maybe another finalist has a book about exactly the topic that everyone on the committee agreed at lunch was a topic they really needed to find. Perhaps the event planner felt that she's had too many white male speakers, and this year her organization has been asking for a more diverse speaker roster. The bottom line is: who knows! The point is that you can't just hang around outside waiting and waiting for each decision – you've got to just keep on keeping on and filling out more and more formal proposals. You can't stop at just one or two.

On the other hand, some speakers utilize innovative nudges when they can for pushing the decision-makers' thinking their way. There's no way to tell whether most of them work, of course, but logic suggests that you at least try some or all of them because . . . well . . . ya just never know! Maybe one of these techniques will push the selection team over the edge, in a good way, i.e., in your favor.

Consider:

1. Have you just published a new article on the topic you're proposing? Try forwarding it to the contact listed on the form. There's usually a contact name and email address for someone.

2. Ditto on #1 if you've landed some good recent publicity and/or a good book review.

3. Has a past sponsor just sent you a pile of evaluations on your most recent gig? If you've come out on top with most of them, send a few of those to the contact person too.

Get the idea? The only caveat is to be careful not to forward so many that it annoys the conference contact. One or two maybe? Three or four? Spaced apart once a week perhaps? It's a tough judgment call to make, but try your best and do whatever feels like common sense. It just may make a difference.

Finding the Right Conferences

The arrival of Google and any similarly effective search engine has certainly made this hunt easier than it used to be. Before the advent of the Internet you had to drag yourself to a library and haul out heavy tomes from the reference section, massive volumes laden with thousands of listings of professional associations that annually sponsor conferences, and perhaps smaller regional and local events too.

Of course you can still do it this way, and you don't necessarily have to trek off to your library either. Many of these volumes are available for sale or via annual subscription both in print and online. Some of the best known include www.associationexces.com (online) and the National Trade and Professional Associations Directory (in print).

But with the Internet you can wring out results just by entering a variety of keywords and seeing what happens. Eventually you're bound to come up with at least a few organizations that seem to fit the kind of speaking you want to do.

Say you want to speak to finance clubs in the Houston area about new software you've developed that helps financial advisors keep track of their clients' assets, and you have some tips you can offer in addition. Maybe your topic is titled "Five Mistakes Advisors Make When Working with Clients . . . and How to Correct Them!"

Open Google, type in your target audience (financial advisors), city name (Houston), type of event (conferences or business events), dates for the next 6 to 12 months (June to December 2017), and so forth. Try various combinations of these criteria and see what happens. Before long you'll find just what you're looking for. If not, maybe you're barking up the wrong tree. There may not be any events of the kind you've been looking for, so you change your criteria a bit (insurance brokers, perhaps) and take another crack at it.

I suggest as well that you enter your search data into an Excel spreadsheet, Google Docs grid, or some other information-capturing software to create what I call a *detail grid*. You'll want to capture as much essential information as possible so that you don't forget or misplace it later on. Significant details include the name of the conference or event, date of same, sponsoring organization, speaker proposal guidelines link, deadline for speaker proposals, contact name and email, topic you proposed, your answers to critical questions, and so forth.

This step will help you keep track of everything that you need. This is a must if you're truly going to do this right, i.e., play the numbers game by filling out as many proposals as you can. When a favorable response comes, months after you've filled out the online proposal form, it will help considerably to have a system in place that will instantly refresh your memory. That way you'll know what you proposed and how you answered specific questions, so that you can respond intelligently to requests from event planners for "a little more information" to help them finalize their decision. The detail grid you've constructed may spell the difference between winning and losing the gig. Fumbling around trying to recall what you had proposed and to whom is not a winning strategy.

Extra Careful Vetting

One important caveat to keep in mind is the need to carefully vet any events or conferences you come across during your search. This may mean looking at them at least a few times. At first glance an event may *seem* to be right for you, but upon a second or third glance it may not. For example:

1. Who will be attending this event? Is this audience one you really want to speak to? I often look for a management consultant audience since that's always been a good fit for me. But if I stumble across a business trade show I could mistakenly, in the thrill of the initial aha! moment, assume that consultants will be there.

    Then when I look closely at the membership demographics of this organization or the "Who Should Attend" section, I realize that attendees will more likely be managers of retail stores, insurance sales reps, and real estate brokers. And the speakers from last year's program, often listed on the conference website, are all from these same industries.

    Thus, if I had skipped ahead to the proposal form and filled it out without any further vetting, I would likely have been wasting my time . . . even if I had been selected!

2. A second type of extra careful vetting would be to study the speaker guidelines for such red flags as: "all speakers are expected to pay their own expenses to this event" or "speakers will not be allowed to make their books available for sale" (yes, amazingly, you sometimes see this) or – how about this one – "all speakers are expected to register for the conference at the regular conference rate." In other words, for the privilege of traveling at your own expense, reserving two or three days of your time, preparing a *customized* presentation for hours beforehand, and then putting on a

rousing good show for the education and enjoyment of the attendees, in return for doing all of this . . . you pay them!

The height of both arrogance and ungraciousness perhaps? I would say so, yes.

3. One other crucial vetting is to check speaker guidelines, past agendas, and future agendas for the kinds of topics being sought. Otherwise you may be proposing yourself for a party to which you would never, under any circumstances, be invited!

   Many events only bring in speakers who are members of the sponsoring organizations, for example. Or they choose only speakers knowledgeable about industry-specific issues, skill-building for their particular professions, trends in their industry, or new policies and regulations on the horizon. In other words, they have no interest in a speaker who will teach them, as in my case, how to write and publish a book. Such a topic is outside the focus for these kinds of events.

SPEAKER NOTES

Steve Markman of Markman Speaker Management says, "Follow up continuously and persistently with the event organizer to help you and your company stay above the noise, since you will often be competing with several other speakers or companies for the same speaking slot."

Words of Warning

Beyond careful vetting, I have a few caveats that are useful to keep in mind when you're seeking out new gigs.

1. **Don't hide your book if you have one!** Make sure the phrase "author of (insert book title)" follows your name immediately in your bio and in the body of your speaking topic blurb and intro so that it can't be missed. Many speakers bury mention of their book deep in their bio or blurb . . . or fail to mention it at all! Don't do this! Don't hide your book – make sure it's impossible to miss.

2. **Include a glowing testimonial or a link to your impressive publicity!** There may be a box for additional comments or information. If so, don't just leave that box blank – use it to slip in a testimonial or publicity link. But if no such box exists, locate another box – maybe the one for your bio, blurb, or learning objectives – to insert a glowing testimonial or link to some impressive publicity. But by all means find somewhere to put these in. You've got to use all your guns, because you're only going to get off one good shot.

3. **It's OK to apply to RFPs,** but be judicious! RFPs (requests for proposals) are usually a bad idea because the competition can be very stiff since they're being sent out to who-knows-how-many potential applicants. However, if something seems like a *perfect* fit for you, go ahead and give it a try. But RFPs typically demand the most exhausting volume and level of responses from applicants,

so if you fill out too many of them you'll be spending *all* your time on them . . . literally. So don't go overboard; stick to the other tactics discussed in this book.

And by the way, that goes double for speaker-wanted ads. The competition will be tough here too with so many competitors jockeying for just one slot. Only one out of a hundred, or one out of a thousand, or one out of ten thousand will get the gig. Obviously there are better ways to spend your time than this, so don't be seduced by this devilishly alluring tempter.

4. **Frequently, conferences want you, the speaker, to pay them to let you speak** under the sneaky guise of the conference registration fee. But if all you want to do is run in, do your thing, then bustle away, you probably won't have to pay a registration fee. Most conference planners will at least grant you the favor of not charging you for your presentation.

   But should you wish to attend the full conference or a part of it, including staying around after your presentation, perhaps for lunch or to attend a breakout or two, many conferences respond "uh-uh." To do this you'll have to pay the same amount as other attendees, usually the highest non-member rate by the way.

   You might not object so much to this if you're already a member of the sponsoring organization, or if you work in the industry or profession that the conference addresses.

I once accepted this arrangement when I was actively involved with the Institute of Management Consultants. As a member-activist, I understood that our conference budget was very limited and that we were close to our break-even point. Since I was deeply involved in IMC, I didn't mind contributing to the cause. Speaking for free and paying to attend the conference seemed fair given that I would have paid to attend anyhow. Getting to speak, in this context, was a bonus for me, not a rip-off.

However, whenever we on the board at IMC invited a speaker to come in from the outside to share some knowledge and expertise that might be of great use to our members, it seemed only right, fair, and hospitable to pay their expenses and an honorarium too, if we could. But certainly we could at least waive our conference fee. After all, it didn't cost us much to allow the speaker to hang out with us, sip a coffee, and fill up a plate at the buffet table. Beyond that, our invited guest speaker was only going to stroll around, chat, and take a seat in the audience to experience other speakers. I mean, really, why not?

To insist on a full registration fee, or to expect even a discounted speaker registration fee, just seems petty. Or even, yes, outright greedy. It's also counterproductive to making the conference the best experience for attendees that it could possibly be. Allowing a speaker to attend the full conference, or at least part of it, before she or he actually speaks can only be to the attendees' advantage.

The speaker, by networking, chatting with attendees, and experiencing other speakers and sitting through their Q&A sessions, can't help but soak up customized knowledge! That then translates into a more informed speaker with a more in-tune presentation.

So be aware of what you're getting into if you're accepted for an event that might end up costing you money. You might choose to go for it anyhow if the attendee demographics offer you potential consulting or training business. But if not, with so many other opportunities out there, the smart move might be to skip this one and just move on.

Checking Event Demographics

When it comes to checking the demographics of your potential audience, I can tell you from sad, personal experience that it's important to check multiple times before you accept any gig. I failed to do this once and regretted it big time.

I'd been accepted to speak at an educator's conference in Washington, DC, and I was beyond excited, until I noticed the fine print specifying that neither a speaking fee nor travel expenses would be included. I wasn't happy, obviously, but, hey, maybe it would be worth the trip down on my own dime from Boston to DC anyway. After all, it was a major conference of educators, right? Wouldn't such a professional group be interested in learning how to publishing a book? Publish or perish, right? I packed my bags and headed to Logan Airport.

When I reached the conference, however, I noticed that my audience of "educators" emanated less from the professorial side of things and more from the ranks of bureaucracy. Administrators and teacher's aides filed into the little room where my presentation was to be held, at 3 p.m. on a Friday afternoon by the way, not my favorite time to gear up for a rousing performance! But I was a pro and the show must go on.

I slogged my way through it all, but in the back of my mind the whole time was the thought that I really should have checked the demographics more carefully. What percentage of "educator attendees" would have any interest at all in what I had to say about getting their book idea published, and, of those who did, would any of them be in a position to hire me to help them do so?

Though I don't mind doing pro bono presentations now and then, I wasn't crazy about shelling out so much time and money to do so.

By not carefully vetting how close this event's attendee demographics were to my target audience, I ended up feeling very discouraged on the plane ride home. I resolved then and there that I would never make that colossal mistake again.

CHAPTER SEVEN

Making Informal Proposals

The truth is there are more leads than you would
ever, in your lifetime, have time to follow up.

> — CATHLEEN FILLMORE, *The Six-Figure
> Speaker* (Robert D. Reed Publishers)

SOME YEARS AGO I participated in a panel at the CEO Club of
Boston, addressing the topic "Innovative Marketing Ideas for
Your Business." My piece of course focused on publishing articles
and books in order to position your business (and its CEO) as a
thoughtleader. Meanwhile my colleague, speaker placement consultant Steve Markman, explained in detail the pros and cons of
speaking engagements. A third panelist, who specialized in traditional public relations, discussed the media.

The three of us had come together because Steve had reached
out to Fred W. Green, the chairman of the CEO Club of Boston,
just by picking up the phone and introducing himself, then asking Fred if he would be interested in a program of this kind. Fred

listened, felt it was a good idea, and set up a meeting with the three of us to work out the details.

Fred hadn't required an online proposal form to be filled out, hadn't placed an ad in a business newspaper seeking speakers, and hadn't even bothered to post a need for speakers on his website. But Steve knew that Fred was open to speaker candidates for his meetings, so he took a chance and called him cold. Then it was simply a matter of sealing the deal.

Making informal proposals to speak works just like that. You think about or hear about a group that sponsors speakers on a regular basis and, if the group's demographics equal your target audience, you send an email or you make a call to the event planner who handles such things. This won't always result in a gig or even a response, of course, but more often than you might expect, it will.

Following that initial speaking gig at the CEO Club, it occurred to me that a roomful of CEOs was a place where I should probably continue to show up. It would be great to speak there again if I could make that happen. Why should I presume that I'd had my one and only shot and that would be the end of it? So I reached out to Fred on my own, now that I knew him and he had seen what I could do – and offered him a deal he couldn't refuse.

Meeting him for lunch a few weeks after the program (upon my suggestion, of course, making it clear beforehand that I was buying!), I proposed that we set up an in-kind partnership. "I'll help you promote the CEO Club by getting articles published about it and media attention. I'll also inform you when a client of mine has a book coming out so that you can invite them to speak to the club if you think their topic is a good fit. In return you let me attend club meetings at no charge so that I can enjoy your other speakers, do some networking, and perhaps pick up a client or two now and then." I assured him I wouldn't be pushy, only collegial. It wasn't my intention to bother or pressure any of his members.

Fred liked this arrangement and said yes to it immediately. It wouldn't cost him anything save for allowing me to partake of the breakfast buffet and coffee. He had set up a similar arrangement with an audio expert so that CDs could be made of each meeting's presentations. So what did he have to lose?

I have since spoken multiple times to the CEO Club and pitched many of my clients to Fred as potential speakers. Happily he has accepted many of them. I also offered Fred free copies of my book *The Expert's Edge* to give out as speaker gifts. That saves Fred the cost of purchasing such gifts and affords me an additional small way to (subtly) market myself to the CEO members.

Fred Green is a prime example of how the informal process of obtaining speaking engagements can work. Because Fred and I have built a close relationship over the years, we understand each other and thus are able to give each other help and support as needed. Fred has also come to understand intimately what I do and therefore never holds back recommending me to club members who could use my help. I've picked up quite a few excellent clients thanks to his endorsements.

Our arrangement is a boon for Fred in his role as event planner. He considers both Steve and me speaker brokers and appreciates the way we've made his job easier. "You guys make things easier by taking care of details, responding to me quickly, making sure your speaker shows up on time, and so forth." He can't say that, he adds, for many speakers' reps or managers, nor for speakers themselves, nor for speakers bureaus.

"Let me speak to the speaker directly too," he explains, "otherwise I may get stuck if a rep from a speakers bureau or management firm suddenly leaves her job, and her replacement doesn't know who I am. Just introduce me to the speaker and then get out of the way. Life for an event planner like me is a lot easier that way."

An added bonus of an informal arrangement like this is that the relationship with one event planner spills over into more such gigs with other event planners. In Fred's case, since his CEO Club of Boston is one of a group of CEO Clubs, in cities such as Dallas, Baltimore, and New York, our arrangement has resulted in additional gigs for my clients and me. In Dallas I once enjoyed a long lunch and tour of the neighborhood with Chairman John Brown while I was there to speak to the Dallas/Ft. Worth chapter of the Institute of Management Consultants. It made perfect sense for me to use the occasion of this IMC gig (expenses paid!) to piggyback a meeting with a CEO Club director to launch a working relationship. That, my friends, is how you grow your informal speaking network!

Making the Approach

The informal proposal process doesn't require filling out an online proposal form or any other formal proposal or application. It merely requires reaching out to an event planner or to someone who might be able to introduce you to a planner, and then making your pitch.

The best way to begin is with an email, I believe, because so many of us prefer that means of initial communication. It's a great way to get many, many pitches out in a short period of time, whereas cold calls can bog you down when someone actually picks up the phone, isn't really in the market for what you're selling . . . but loves to chat! That might seduce you into chatting a while with them in the hopes of changing their mind, but it risks your losing a good hour or so on someone who was never going to say yes in the first place. So instead I opt for emails first, and then, if you get even a nibble, you can email back and suggest a phone call . . . now that you've got a fish on the line! Know that the informal process, just as much as the formal process, is a numbers game.

So compose a brief email to get things started – and I do mean brief! Get to the point quickly, followed by a suggestion for further action.

Let's suppose someone referred you to a group called Sales Reps of America. You drop your mutual contact's name right away of course, then structure the rest of your email this way:

Hello Mr. Blue

One of your members, Bob MacDuff, suggested that I contact you about speaking at one of your Sales Reps of America chapter events. Bob thought my experience and insights might be of value to your members and program attendees. I'm a veteran professional sales expert and also author of the book *Selling: You Can Too!*

My speaking topics include "The Art of the Close," "10 Mistakes Most Sales Reps Make," and "How Selling Can Be Fun!" I'm sure that I could help many of your members since I've helped many other sales reps at other groups and companies. I'm good with veteran sales reps too, by the way, not just neophytes. You can learn more about my ability to improve rates of selling success by visiting my website: www.improveselling.com.

Would you like to speak with me about this? If so, I'd be honored to do so, by phone or a visit to your office. Just let me know which works best for you.

And thanks in advance for your attention. I do appreciate it.

Best regards,

George Jackson
Sales Expert, Author, Speaker
Improve Selling Associates

You can see that this email format follows the KISS rule: Keep It Simple, Stupid. No dumping of overwhelming marketing kits or books, no lengthy topic outlines or company case studies. Less is more when it comes to pitching yourself as a speaker during this initial step of the informal proposal process. Just give event planners the chance to read your introduction and then indicate if they wish to make the next move. Which, by the way, might look something like this:

Thank you, George, for these speaking ideas. Yes, we might have a need for a speaker with your expertise.

Could we talk sometime on the phone next week?

For that matter, would you be available to come in and speak to our group on April 4 at our 6–8 p.m. meeting? A speaker I had lined up for that date just backed out on me today!

Please let me know. Thanks.

William Blue, Director
Sales Reps of America, Topeka KS chapter

Sound too easy? Well, sometimes it can work exactly like this! Remember what happened when I called around (pre-email era) and happened upon that diversity event planner (see Chapter Two).

Though I can't guarantee you this kind of response every time, it does happen since this is a numbers game. If you send out enough emails you'll likely get at least a few responses like this. Just make sure that you're sending to your targeted group. If this is going to work for you, you want to ensure that you land exactly the kind of speaking gigs you want.

Speaking Inside Companies

Another venue for speaking gigs is inside a company. I did quite a lot of this at one point in my speaking career. It was easy for me to get these gigs because of my acquaintance with Kathy Greer. An Employee Assistance Program (EAP) consultant whose client list included quite a few mid-size firms, Kathy typically offered her client companies free lunchtime speakers as a bonus feature of her contracts with them. I had originally met her at a monthly networking lunch sponsored by Kathy herself, an opportunity for her and all who attended to meet and get to know other professionals, thus building everyone's business networks so they could trade leads, contacts, and resources to help each other.

Kathy was essentially the keynoter every month at these lunches. Sometimes she would have a guest speaker, but even then she was the emcee. (I'll have more on this speaking format in Chapter Eight, "Creating Your Own.")

After lunching with Kathy one day, all the better to amplify my business relationship with her, she told me about her lunchtime offerings and then wondered if I might be interested in being added to her roster. Payment was either minimal or nonexistent (seriously, I can't remember, it's been quite a few years!), but I could see the value of doing such speaking gigs for the exposure, the practice, and, who knows, any corporate contacts that might develop as I shuffled from company to company. I mean, you just have to get out there!

So I volunteered for one such gig to see how it might go, and since it went well I volunteered again, so that before long I was heading out almost daily to Kathy's gigs and, frankly, loving it. My topics varied sufficiently so that I didn't get bored or stale, and most of these lunchtime audiences gave me their complete attention; I wasn't competing with tuna and chicken salad sandwiches. One time I attracted such a large crowd that people were streaming down the halls and jamming themselves through the door to see me – there may have been 100 or so. I was conducting a motivation session, including music to move to, and by the climax of the session a couple dozen employees were literally dancing on the cafeteria tabletops! It was quite a thrill!

I can't offer any special lessons on how to get these gigs, except to advise you again to network, network, network. Then you too might stumble upon such an opportunity. It just pays to get yourself out there – that's one of the best ways for making things happen. Ya just never know.

In terms of how to more systematically land inside-company gigs, however, some great advice comes from Lois Creamer, a speaker consultant and National Speaker Association member. Lois works with professional speakers who want to "book more business, make more money, and fully monetize their intellectual property." Appropriately, her website is www.bookmorebusiness. com.

Lois's article "Book More Business in 2016," in the January/February 2016 issue of *Speaker Magazine,* advises speakers to "ask for the VP of sales [because] about 80 percent of the time, he/she is the decision-maker." Should this turn out to not be the case, proceed to the VP of marketing next, she says. When you call, look for one of three possible scenarios:

1. **You get the VP on the phone.** This is a good development because you can tell him or her why you're calling and find out, right there and then, if this company ever brings in speakers. "If yes, discuss," Lois writes. If not, move on.

2. **You get his or her assistant.** Should this happen, treat the assistant exactly like you'd treat the VP. "Remember,

these people are very powerful and can many times make decisions . . . make them part of the process."

3. **You get voicemail.** Lois advises you to leave a message with your name, an impact message, the reason that you're calling, and an invitation to call back. Add that you can send something that explains your topic but that you don't want to bother them, so please either call back (Lois's suggestion) or email back (my suggestion).

I always end a voice message such as this one with: "I'll also email what I've just said here after I hang up in case that's more convenient for you to respond to me." I've found that this works great for either getting a simple no so that I can move on or a tentative yes, often including details about what I should do next. So very many of us today (me included) just hate to return a phone call when an email will work just as well. Email allows me to communicate quickly and not get trapped on the phone for an hour or more with a motor mouth. There's only so much time in one day, right?

On the other hand, cold calling, as Lois suggests, can work when it's done right. At a time when people are bombarded by pitches via email, snail mail, pop-ups, Facebook alerts, instant messaging, bing-bing-bing, a phone call remains the most personal and effective way of making contact. So a phone call with a follow-up email is a sensible marketing tactic.

In her book *The Six-Figure Speaker,* Cathleen Fillmore tells the story of Derrick, a speaker who early on accepted the fact that, as a speaker he was also automatically in sales:

In the first couple of years starting out, Derrick set himself the goal of having 25 conversations with prospective clients each day. When calling companies, he had a simple script that went, "Maybe you can help me out. I'm a speaker. Whom should I speak to about upcoming conferences?" That person was sometimes head of HR, or a corporate meeting planner. Now Derrick gets enough business from referrals and bureau bookings that he hasn't had to make so many phone calls.

"So many speakers think they're movie stars when they're not," Derrick says. "They're in sales and they have to make those 25 phone calls per day. This is not always a glamorous occupation!"

Locating the Economic Buyer

Another point to keep in mind is to remember to locate the *economic buyer*. Ask for the VP of sales or whatever, but when you find yourself on the phone with him or her, ask questions that will determine whether this person is the one who will make the final buying decision when it comes to *paying you* for your speaking services. A relentless advocate of this approach is Alan Weiss, a Certified Speaking Professional (CSP) and one of the most sought-after business speakers in the United States (and elsewhere) today.

In his masterful, bestselling book *Million Dollar Speaking*, Weiss maintains that if we speakers fail to identify and speak with the economic buyer, we'll often end up completely wasting our time. "The buyer is the key, and speakers often don't have a clue about the true buyer," he writes in his book. "A buyer is someone who can authorize a check . . . is usually near the top of the hierarchy in smaller organizations, and can be anywhere in larger ones. Titles are deceiving."

Weiss goes on to advise that we should, "[w]henever possible, market and sell to economic buyers," which means understanding that event planners are often *not* economic buyers but mere *feasibility or implementation* buyers. This means that they are typically doled out a strict budget by the economic buyer and told to conserve it. Only economic buyers can offer real reward, Weiss warns, commensurate with your true value.

How do you go about finding these elusive economic buyers? Weiss has it figured out: "My economic buyers have had titles like director, manager, business process consultant, vice president, and, of course, CEO." To ferret out (Weiss's words) the true economic buyer, employ such questions as "Whose budget is supporting this investment?" "Whose objectives are at stake?" "Who approves the final agenda?" and Weiss's personal, straight-to-the-point favorite, "Are you the one investing the money?"

Navigating your way past a feasibility or implementation buyer to the true economic buyer will prove invaluable, because "no risk, no reward. It's simply that important to find the economic buyer and secure your agreement with him or her because only that person can appreciate your value package and the long-term results for the organization in terms of an appropriate investment."

SPEAKER NOTES

Wisdom from Paul Goldner: "How to Obtain High-Profile Clients," sponsored by SpeakerNet News, February 19, 2015:

"The most efficient way to go after companies is to get them to bring you in multiple times. IBM software group alone has 7,500 reps in the United States, thousands more in Asia and the United Kingdom, etc. So I do keynote addresses to all those divisions. Such a "large account strategy" gives you a consistent revenue stream from year to year.

"Prospects are not all created equal . . . proximity to your customer enhances your chances of closing a sale. As the largest company in New York State, IBM is therefore my #1 prospect.

"Make objective decisions about where you spend your time. . . . I use employee count as my statistic to know because it is easy to measure. . . . I target super-large companies with an employee count of 1,000 or more . . . all this info is contained in Hoover's Info . . . go online and download employee count info.

"I call the president of a company or the CEO . . . if you start with a low level like HR, it's hard to ratchet up to CEO. But it's easy to go down from CEOs! Also, the higher you call, the more likely it is to get a return call.

"If you are looking for large accounts, somewhere along the line you have to develop a personal relationship . . . email is fine but you cannot avoid talking to them if you want to give speeches. You have to talk to them, get to know them . . . so just pick up the phone and call!

"I try to make 20 outbound calls a day . . . I make calls before I go out, during lunch, during breaks, etc. . . . How fast or slow do you want to grow your business? I'm committed to success . . . that's why I make the calls."

CHAPTER EIGHT

Creating Your Own Gigs

Life is a do-it-yourself project.

— NAPOLEON HILL, author of *Think and Grow Rich*

IN ADDITION TO PUTTING YOURSELF UP for speaking slots at professional associations and companies, how about creating and sponsoring events of your own? Think of it: no more haggling with event planners, no more filing formal proposals, no more asking around for leads from informal connections and sources. Just set up your own event and "hire" yourself as the speaker.

Which is not to say that there won't be a few issues to overcome when you strike out on your own, but they'll be very different from the kinds of challenges we've been discussing so far in this book. But as with self-publishing your book instead of seeking out a traditional publisher, sponsoring your own event is an endeavor that you're in complete control of, one where you'll sink or swim without needing anyone's permission or life jacket. Work hard enough at it and I promise you this: many great gigs will be the result.

CareerScape

In the years before I founded my present company, emerson consulting, my (now) wife Barbara and I decided to create a self-help career program that we named CareerScape. Its purpose was to guide and empower mid-life professionals through career transition issues. With our help they could take some carefully considered, if at times risky, steps to radically change their careers, modify their careers, or, if this option made the most sense to them at the time, stay in the career they were already in. Over the course of about 10 years we served 8,000 to 10,000 professionals with our program and its customized strategies and advice.

Our format was not the usual one-on-one career counseling approach, although we did offer some of that if a new client felt more comfortable that way. We offered a process in which *career explorers* would work together in a team setting to help each other, with our input, as they faced the challenge of moving themselves into entirely new work lives, or at the very least, new attitudes toward their work.

To pull this off we needed to rent a meeting space for our programs that would accommodate 10 or 12 participants, and sometimes many more. Some of our programs attracted audiences of 50 or more. We also had to develop program registration forms, program workbooks, promotional fliers, and all manner of other program and marketing materials. In terms of our core services, we needed to plan our programs carefully from beginning to end, customizing such planning according to whether program attendees were meeting for an intensive full weekend or for our standard one-evening-a-week, nine-week format. We also had to establish timelines for starting and ending each program and for breaks and lunch hours. Then there was publicity and networking to be done to spread the word to our target markets, a newsletter to send out to our clients, vendors to be obtained . . . really a *lot* that always had to be done.

Was it worth all that time and trouble? Yes, it was, because this was our core business. The path for us to making the most profit was to peddle our career-helping wares in the form of training sessions, something we had to do by ourselves since we were the ones who knew how our CareerScape program worked.

We delivered what were basically shorter sample sessions by partnering with adult education schools, job training organizations, colleges, business training workshops, nonprofits, and professional conferences. But 90 percent of our efforts were composed of our own programs, organized and controlled by us.

This is what I mean by *creating your own:* conceiving, organizing, promoting, and implementing speaking engagements and training programs that are dependent upon no one but yourself. Anyone can do this. But the first question to ask is whether you're up to such an all-out commitment, or if you'd rather not be bothered. That's a big decision.

The decision to create your own can start off very humbly, and this was true of our CareerScape programs. As you attempt to spread the good word about what you have to offer, you might find the public slow to react, slow to see the value you're offering, and even slower to write you out a check!

But if you keep at it you might incrementally build your visibility and reputation. Your program graduates may return to your follow-up sessions again and again as well as tell their friends how great your programs are. In some cases they might even drag them along to a program of yours. If you can hang on long enough, this dynamic will one day fill up your space with audiences that are hanging on your every word.

My current business emphasizes direct and customized consultation services for our clients. Thus it was years before I decided to offer a one-day session called "Thoughtleading Launchpad," and later another called "Publishing Your Ideas." Because this was a new fit for me, would-be participants didn't exactly break down my door, although I did manage to enroll the half dozen or so that I had hoped for from the beginning.

In one session though, enrollments were nonexistent, but instead of cancelling the program altogether I offered six $795 tickets to clients and colleagues whom I knew would appreciate attending and who might help spread the word to friends and colleagues who would be willing to pay the advertised fee. This sometimes is the route you have to take to build a business in which your speaking engagements are conducted totally under your own control.

Bottom line here? Yes, it can be done.

Sponsoring Yourself
at an Important Venue

A variation that also fits the definition of *creating your own* is to shell out a few bucks for a sponsorship at an important event, i.e., one that's aimed at your target audiences. This might be a professional association or corporate meeting, or even a nonprofit fundraising or charitable event. The idea would be that they will be doing all the organizing and heavy lifting, which frees you up to simply write them a check and show up at the appointed time to do your thing.

You might find that the price you pay for a sponsorship approximates what you might spend had you done it all on your own. Thus you might consider it worth the price if you view it as delegating all the work that you would've had to spend time on yourself. Another advantage is that this organization you're sponsoring already has a following of some sort, and a mailing list, an email list, a membership list, hundreds or thousands of former attendees, etc., all of whom might be willing to come this time just to see *you*. Followings of this sort are invaluable because they can take years to amass. So riding the coattails of such organizations can prove very wise indeed. Why instead should you try to re-invent the wheel?

A marketing VP for a major firm told me recently that her company spent a hefty amount every year to sponsor an annual conference of a major executive association. This sponsorship fee allowed her firm's CEO thoughtleader to deliver a keynote to the attending corporate decision-makers. "And the reason we do it," she told me, "is simple: the ROI is tremendous!"

Keep in mind that not all sponsorships result in a tit-for-tat arrangement, where you pay a certain amount and get to deliver a presentation in an enviable speaking slot. In fact, the sponsored organization may not let you deliver any presentations at all!

Many organizations, like publications, want to be careful to maintain a certain level of integrity so that they're not perceived as selling off their resources. If they did so, you and I might decide that this professional group can't be trusted to have *our* best interests at heart, that such a group was merely selling its resources and spotlight to the highest bidder. For this reason, a sponsorship may or may not earn you a speaking slot, so ask the right questions and know what answers you want to hear before you fork over a sponsorship fee.

On the other hand, if your message and information are properly vetted by the organization you're thinking of sponsoring, i.e., if you truly offer the event's attendees something of value, your willingness to help out with a sponsorship fee may get you an exception to the general rule. When I was president of the New England chapter of IMC USA, for example, we put on a one-day conference each year at which we included a trade show, where sponsors could buy a booth or table space to display their marketing materials and chat with attendees during the breaks. Though we didn't automatically offer a speaking slot with a trade show fee, we weren't opposed to approaching a trade show sponsor and offering them such a slot if we determined that their product or service might translate into a "top ten tips presentation" of useful knowledge for our management consultant attendees. Examples of who we deemed would offer genuinely useful information included a newsletter designer, a website developer, a seller of project timeline software, a marketer of an electronic presentation tool, and a representative of a personal finance service.

SPEAKER NOTES

One thing sponsors *should* get, even if it's not always offered, is the chance to speak for a minute or two to the main group about their services or products. If that opportunity isn't offered, it's perfectly appropriate for you to request it. Make sure that the event planners understand that their sponsors have some value to offer the event's attendees and that they should let them make their case. That way the attendees can decide whether their case has been made or not.

And if you're given the opportunity to make a brief presentation, don't wing it! Instead, carefully craft your impact message (refer to Chapter Two) and turn your momentary sponsor spotlight into a mini-keynote!

CHAPTER NINE

Volunteering, Pro Bonos, and Freebies

What's the point of having experience, knowledge, or talent if we never give it away? It is only in giving that we truly connect.

— Isabel Allende, author and recipient of Chile's National Literature Prize and the U.S. Presidental Medal of Freedom

LOVE SPEAKING TO JOB SEARCH SUPPORT GROUPS. I love it because I can introduce their members, mainly unemployed professionals, to job-hunting tactics that will help them find new jobs and position themselves for better jobs in the future.

Too often professionals temporarily out of work cruise through their days with blinders on, focused single-mindedly on finding that next position. That's important, of course, but those blinders can keep you from seeing innovative actions that might prevent you from losing your future job.

For example, viewing yourself as a unique "business" while you're unemployed can open up a sea of possibilities in terms of how to track down and nail that new employer, just as a successful business positions itself as offering a unique value proposition. To beat its competition the business markets itself in such a way that it's positioned head and shoulders *above* its competition in some aspect – the highest quality, the best value, the biggest selection of benefits, the best fit for its customer's need, etc.

Job hunters should be operating in exactly the same way, aping this age-old business marketing strategy. But most job hunters ignore this strategy, often never even considering it. They don't market themselves. Instead they just plod along, hand out or email resumes, network here and there, then wait. When they get a job interview they dutifully answer the interviewer's questions, head home, and start waiting again. If a business did such things, it would soon have to close its doors!

Frequently, and ironically, an out-of-work professional is a veteran with a long, storied career who has gathered many insights over the years. And if such insights can be communicated during a job interview, why can't they be expanded to a 45-minute presentation? So when I speak to a job hunters support group I try to open my new jobless friends' eyes to such possibilities.

By now you may be thinking: How much business would I possibly gain from such a speaking gig? Job hunters have no money, and they won't be quick to part with what they have. So why bother?

The reasons I occasionally speak to such a group are many, but picking up a new client isn't one of them. But that very fact is the key to why speaking to an audience of the unemployed can be viewed as such a good gig . . . because you have nothing to lose!

Speaking to an audience that will never result in new business for you frees you up to use the gig for practice. New presentations, new ideas, new jokes, new interactive audience games, all these potential additions to your regular presentations integrate better after you try them out and practice them. Speaking to a live audience when there's not much at stake serves you so much better than practicing alone in front of a mirror or video camera. Practicing before real people is kinetic, unpredictable, enlivening, and real.

Stand-up comics do it all the time. I once spied the late Robin Williams chatting unobtrusively with a small group in the bar area of a New York City comedy club. He wasn't on the bill for that evening. The lineup instead consisted of about eight unknown, and fairly mediocre, comics. At about 3 a.m., when most of the patrons had left, Robin came on without fanfare and did a few bits. Some of them were funny, some were awkward. I was told later that he had quietly come to the club that night to try out new routines, some of which worked and some of which didn't. He would toss out the stuff that didn't work. If such a practice is good enough for a superstar like Robin Williams, why wouldn't it make sense for you and me?

How to get booked: If you search online for groups of job hunters in your area, you'll likely stumble across a few to approach.

Many times these groups meet in a church hall or some other free venue. Most likely you'll be met with open arms from the job group's organizer – since they can't pay they appreciate any offers to donate services.

When you're there ask the organizer or even the group if they know of other groups you could speak to. More than likely they will, but don't expect other groups they propose to offer paying gigs. But on the other hand, ya just never know. These folks may be unemployed, but they were employed once upon a time and will be again. They may be members (if they're smart) of a professional association of some kind. So it obviously wouldn't hurt to ask.

Rotary Clubs

Another pro bono venue is your local Rotary club. These audiences are made up of business folks from the Rotary's city or town or region. It's always possible that some kind of business that fits the bill for you might come your way. But your main motivation for speaking at a Rotary club is that it's an opportunity to practice and refine your material before you go out to a group where you have more to lose. Many speakers who try this venue, thinking it might be good for their business, end up very frustrated, reporting that their Rotary audience didn't seem fully engaged. But that challenge provides great practice for you as a speaker rather than a reason to stay away. If you can capture that crowd's attention and then hold on to it and ride it home, you'll be teaching yourself to grab hold of virtually any crowd! As Rodney Dangerfield used to say, "Tough crowd, tough crowd. I can't get no respect." Yes, that's just how many speakers feel upon completing a Rotary gig, and it's precisely why you should speak to them.

So why are Rotary audiences so tough? Here are my conclusions:

1. Rotary clubs require their members to attend meetings every week. Members who are ill or traveling on business or vacation are expected to somehow find a way to make up those missed meetings. Maybe they could achieve this by attending a meeting in the city in which they are vacationing, or perhaps attend a second meeting the week they come home (or recover from illness) in a neighboring town. But attendance 52 times a year is encouraged, expected, and even mandated.

2. This perfect attendance rule impacts you, the Rotary speaker, in that many in your audience may not be interested in what you have to say. They haven't come to hear you talk about your topic, but to socialize and fulfill the attendance requirement. And to have some lunch! So as soon as you begin speaking it's time for some of them to start glancing at their watch, and when you're finished many will bolt out the door and scurry back to work. When your 20 minutes are up, which is all the time you'll get, that week's meeting is so over.

3. Finally, many in the room have been in business for a long, long time, so they've heard it all before, or they feel like they have. This means you'll have to work hard to offer

something that will wow these grizzled, possibly burned-out, veterans.

On the bright side, they may give you a nice Rotary speaker gift such as a fountain pen, book, or pedometer, and . . . they'll be courteous. Also, if you're really good, someone may actually pop up afterward and suggest that you come and speak to another business group that they're part of. Maybe that one will offer more potential for follow-on business or even a paid speaking gig.

How to get booked: Start with the Rotary in your own town. Show up at a meeting and offer to pay your way that day, explaining that you just want to check it out. Or ask someone you know who's a member to bring you in as a guest. Once in the inner sanctum, say hi to the current program chair and offer your services. It could be that simple.

You can also check out your state Rotary club website and pick up other Rotary contacts to email or call. Before long you'll be tooling up and down nearby highways and byways to Rotaries of all sizes and stripes!

SPEAKER NOTES

Chambers of Commerce are also great venues for tackling tough crowds, and they might potentially lead to business. Though Chambers can have membership demographics that are similar to Rotaries, their members tend to be less bored by speakers. Since Chambers don't have perfect-attendance rules, many members come to hear specific speakers and topics rather than because they have to. The only issue in trying to get gigs at Chambers is that some require speakers to be members of that particular Chamber or to speak on legal and government topics, such as changing business regulations. But assuming you get the gig, your topic will probably be more listened to than at a Rotary club meeting and therefore more satisfying to both you and your Chamber audience.

Program Committees

Any speaking engagement can potentially lead you to more and better gigs down the road, so it never hurts to advertise yourself by getting out and speaking wherever and whenever you can. The more you speak the more likely it becomes that someone will pass your name along with a ringing endorsement, which could place you up on a podium at a grand event of some kind, perhaps even as a conference keynote. So be sure to keep plugging all your audience attendees into your e-list, including those currently unemployed.

Another pro bono opportunity typically stares speakers in the face and they don't even notice it. There's probably a professional organization populated by your target market and referral sources. Join it. Attend their meetings and, if you can, get actively involved. Committee members or directors are always welcome!

Do engineering firms typically hire you? How about high-tech collaboratives? Where do their decision-makers congregate? Maybe there's a high-technology council in your area, or a state chapter of the American Engineering Society. If you're a bona fide engineer or IT specialist yourself you could probably join. The idea is to get as close as you can to potential customers, rub shoulders with them month after month, and build up mutually beneficial relationships.

I wrote earlier about how I launched my business via my involvement in a local chapter of IMC USA. That positioned me as a go-to expert for their panel "Writing and Speaking to Advance Your Consulting Practice." So, no fool am I, over the next year I made sure I got *more* involved in IMC – I know a good thing when I see one! – which included joining their program committee.

Though I didn't do this in order to shamelessly self-promote to my new IMC colleagues, it wasn't lost on me that an opportunity to speak again to an IMC audience might emerge if I hung around the program team. By merely making myself present at programming discussions, I might just end up making my own luck.

One morning I joined Brad Hosmer, the program chair, and Brooks Fenno, the chapter president, for a program committee breakfast meeting to discuss speakers for upcoming meetings. A fourth member of the committee, whose name I've long since forgotten, didn't show up, so the three of us made the final decisions.

Brad plopped down a tall stack of papers, which we three ignored for about 30 minutes while we chatted about other things and ordered breakfast. Halfway through the meal Brad explained that his tall stack of material represented proposals he had received over the past few months from hopeful speakers. He said he figured we might go through this forbidding stack and winnow out some of them.

While I berated myself silently with questions such as (a) why hadn't I thought to formally propose *myself* to Brad, and (b) how could I now manage to insert myself into consideration despite all this competition vying for our attention, Brooks suggested there might be a better way to proceed than to spend the time it would take to go through all that material.

"What do our members want to learn about?" Brooks asked. "Can we list five or six topics we would want to find speakers for?" That got us brainstorming about what subject matter made the most sense for our program to address.

Twice during this brainstorming, topics came up that were right up my alley – how to publish a book, how to obtain media publicity for one's consulting practice. I froze, not wanting to appear too forward or grabby. But Brooks lit up each time, blurting out, "Ken could do that one!" and "Ken could do that one, too!" Brad nodded his head in agreement both times, and so did I. "

"Yes I could do that one," I said, trying to sound nonchalant. But I *really* wanted to be selected. We then moved on to other topics and possible speakers, and before long we had settled on speakers and topics for the next six months without even glancing at the tall stack of proposals.

"Great meeting!" we all agreed. As far as Brooks and Brad were concerned, we had accomplished our task.

As for me, I drove away not knowing what had just happened but obviously glad it had. Just by showing up I was starting the day with two new, very good speaking gigs, both with the exact audience venue I most wanted.

Pro Bono Gigs for the RIGHT Audience

I can't conclude this chapter without mentioning what might seem obvious yet perhaps isn't. If your goal is to develop business for your company as a result of your speaking gigs, pro bono will often be the way to go when you land a gig with your target audience. Since you have your sights set on bigger fish than just a one-time speaker fee, why worry about it? Of course if you can get both, then go for it. But if it looks like doing the gig pro bono is your only choice, go for it.

Don't let your ego get in the way by thinking that you *must* be paid for all professional engagements. By speaking to IMC audiences I've gotten many clients over the years. I've been flown to IMC chapters in Texas, Arizona, New Jersey, etc. to speak to their management consultant members, and I've flown out on my own dime to national IMC events, too. In none of these situations have I ever asked about a fee. Travel expenses yes, fee no.

The reason is that IMC chapters, and even the national organization, don't rake in such big bucks that they can afford to pay speaker fees. Many are pushing it to even pay for coach plane fare and a low-budget hotel. But their audiences are the kind I'm looking for, where a lucrative project or client is likely to come my way.

Accepting pro bono gigs in such circumstances works just fine for us all.

You may encounter similar situations at organizations that you might expect would be able to pay but don't. I'm thinking of the many CEO Clubs and Vistage chapters around the country. Many of these organizations don't pay fees, or even expenses, because they don't have to! There's so much competition for these slots because there are more speakers than CEO audiences.

So take the long view when it comes to speaker fees. You can't get one if they can't afford to give you one, and you can't get one if they know they don't have to give you one. If you get rigid about it you'll probably lose out on the other benefits of speaking to your target audience. Giving yourself away is frequently the wisest thing you can do.

CHAPTER TEN

Taking Advantage of People Resources

Help! I need somebody!

— Lyrics from "Help" by The Beatles

ARE YOU TAKING ADVANTAGE OF PEOPLE who will help you locate more and better speaking gigs? Going it alone isn't always the best policy in the speaking business, while getting some help frequently is. You're now more than halfway through this book, an excellent first step. Maybe it's time to take it up a notch. Seeking direct help from competent professionals could significantly optimize your chances further, so let's begin with the most direct help you could possibly imagine: your own speaker manager.

Hiring someone to be your speaker placement manager makes a lot of sense. Comments from successful speakers who have done so include such luminaries as Larry Winget, Suzanne Bates, Duane Cashin, Jim Bouchard, and the author of this book. My own story, in fact, is a good place to start.

I hired Andy Karl some years ago to make contact with event planners and pitch me to them as a speaker for their conferences, training programs, and other needs. Since this was during the early days of the Internet, almost all of Andy's work was done on the phone, but he seemed to prefer it that way. Andy had the proverbial gift of gab, and he wasn't afraid to get on the phone and use it.

I had a tiny office back then, which I had to share with Andy, so I was often in the room when he was making his calls. He had a nice, easy capacity to engage each stranger on the phone, respectfully kibitz with them, and then patiently, subtly, and professionally move the conversation to the event planner's speaking needs, and from there back to me as a speaker the planner should consider.

He was also persistent! He kept at it, doggedly working down his call list, setting up a second phone appointment when a planner indicated initial interest, then following up with marketing materials or additional info when such a step might keep things moving in the right direction. He wasn't good at taking no for an answer.

By the end of six months Andy had come up with a few major gigs that I otherwise would never have known to apply for, much less gotten. One was a training session requested by a corporate manager who wanted someone to come in for half a day and shake up her staff, with the aim of improving her team's motivation and creative thinking.

A second good gig was a keynote address based on a book I had written called *Balancing Work and Family* (AMACOM Books). This keynote would be delivered to the League of Van and Trailer Manufacturers (now defunct) in the very heart of conference speaking land – Las Vegas, Nevada! I got a great speaking fee, airfare and other travel expenses, accommodation at the conference's hotel – the works.

A third good gig, though I hadn't recognized it at the time, was with Harvard University. Andy had stumbled upon an opportunity to conduct two evening workshops for the Harvard University Extension School annual conference, one of them based on that same book. However, big shot that I now was, having keynoted in Vegas and all, I balked at the paltry fee.

"They're only paying $100 per workshop?" I reacted. "I don't think I want to do it for that."

Andy kept his cool and did what a speaker manager should do – he argued with me.

"I think you should take it," he replied. "It's Harvard, after all, and it could lead to other things elsewhere. Look at the credibility you'll gain. And they might want you back there after these two gigs are over, so opportunities could develop right there at Harvard itself."

I thought about it overnight and, once the dust settled over my ego, reluctantly agreed. A few weeks later I conducted both workshops and, to my pleasant surprise, enjoyed them both immensely. The next week they invited me to come back on a regular basis (at the same $100-a-session fee) and deliver career motivation seminars to the Extension School's adult students.

I got into a rhythm driving there once a month, and the next thing I knew I had been making the drive and conducting the same programs for 15 years! My fee gradually rose over the years to $300 per session, but the money wasn't really why I continued. I loved the concept of speaking regularly at Hah-vahd and loved that I could add the Ivy League to my resume and speaker bio. I enjoyed having a post-session burger in Harvard Square and, frankly, I enjoyed the very process of helping these adult students learn effective and innovative strategies for finding a job they would love. So on all fronts, Andy's pushing me turned out to be one of the best things that came out of his work for me. It was a benefit of hiring a speaker manager I could not have predicted.

Others Who Have Done It

The concept of hiring a speaker rep like Andy came to me originally from the enormously successful "pit bull of personal development," Larry Winget. Larry had come to the Boston area many years ago to speak on the topic of how to land speaking engagements at NSA New England (National Speakers Association).

Although I hadn't been able to attend his program, someone gave me a tape he had made of it, and I was so absorbed by all that Larry had to say that I listened to it again and again. When Larry mentioned that he had other recordings (and videos) for sale, I leaped at the chance to learn more from him. In the next few months I absorbed every Larry Winget nugget that I could, all of it drawn from his own experiences and inventive strategies for getting himself up on a stage.

Now, so many years later, I remember his adamant advocacy of hiring a speaker manager. He had pioneered the concept, explaining that it takes a lot of time to make those phone calls, do research, and follow up. You can't do that well in addition to traveling to far-flung events where you'll be way too busy to do anything other than prepare to speak, then speak, then rush to the local airport and fly home.

Similarly, my good friend Suzanne Bates, author of *Speak Like A CEO* and her current book *All the Leader You Can Be* and other books from McGraw-Hill, has employed a speaker manager throughout most of her 15 years building a now-global executive coaching firm. Formerly an award-winning TV news reporter and anchor, Suzanne came to the consulting world already clear about the benefits of speaking in public. She knew the smart way to market herself would be to build upon the notoriety that her television news career had already given her by speaking to as many targeted groups as she could.

To help her with this and other functions, she employed, initially, a part-time assistant to relieve her of much of the nitty-gritty, day-to-day operations that come automatically with the territory. This help was especially useful when she was out networking, building relationships, coaching and consulting with her clients, and of course speaking. As her business grew, she spotted a talented intern whom she developed into a marketing director whose functions included speaker pitching and engagement management. This opened up the possibility of Suzanne speaking at national conferences in addition to the easier-to-get local gigs.

Today Suzanne presides over a firm with 33 employees and associates and corporate clients around the globe, and speaker management is more important than ever. Her marketing team includes an individual with speaker management responsibilities. The usefulness of delegating this function has proven itself and grown in value exponentially since the day Suzanne's business began.

So hire someone to hunker back at your office and pitch you to event planners and make those follow-up emails and phone calls. Your job is to get out there and speak whenever you can to your target audiences.

Outsourcing Options

Though hiring a staffer as your speaker manager may be the right call for you, as it has been for Suzanne, Larry Winget, and others, if your organization is very large, or if those who work for you are stretched very thin, it might make more sense for you to engage an outside speaker management service. This is especially true if your goal is to obtain engagements not only for you but also for one or more of your colleagues or employees. In that case consider outsourcing this function to a high-level speaker (or personal) management service devoted exclusively to obtaining, for a fee, important speaking engagements.

One speaker management service is Markman Speaker Management, founded in 1994 by Steve Markman. Prior to this Steve had worked for The Conference Board as head of its Conference Division, and in a similar position at Comdex, where during this period of his career he learned the nuts and bolts of how conferences come together, including what makes one event successful and another flop. He also observed what a speaker needed to do to be viewed as an asset rather than a liability to a conference or event planner. Steve can now claim to know everything anyone could ever want to know about speaker and event success.

"Standing out from the crowd," he explains, "regardless of your organization's industry, is a huge challenge. But companies need to expose their expertise and technologies to prospective customers and clients, and so they've got to find a way. While it's fine to evaluate unsolicited speaking opportunities in a random fashion as they come in, having someone dedicated to this task and aggressively identifying worthwhile opportunities can be invaluable. Developing relationships with event organizers, and writing and submitting speaker proposals, a professional who knows what he or she is doing will increase the frequency of your winning new speaking engagements, which in turn increases visibility for your participating executives and thus for the firm as a whole."

Armed with such expertise, Steve has served hundreds of corporate and individual speaking clients, handling all details of moving them from topic formulation to actual presentation before an audience. He provides an outsourcing option for obtaining speaking engagements for firms whose needs extend beyond the capacity of an in-house staff member to fill.

I must add one footnote to the discussion of services like Steve's. Unlike a speakers bureau, Steve charges each client a fee. As we noted in Chapter One, a speakers bureau will typically *not* function as your hard-working representative, they will *not* beat the bushes for you day in and day out unless they come across one or more paid speaking opportunities for which you are a definite fit. Instead, look for that kind of service from a personal management firm or a speaker manager or agent, though with the caveat that these services typically focus on both paid and unpaid speaking gigs rather than exclusively paid ones.

The role Andy played for me was to research potential speaking gigs and then pitch me to their event planners or sponsoring conferences. A service such as Steve's will perform this function for you and/or your organization. Because you're paying a fee in both these cases, you're entitled to expect a dedicated effort to obtain for you exactly what you want.

In the case of a bureau, however, you're not paying anything unless a speaking gig is found for you. Such an arrangement motivates the bureau representing you to spend only as much time on your behalf as the market dictates. The inclination is to spend time on those speakers for whom positive responses are coming in, because that's where the money is!

So don't confuse the two different kinds of service. Investing in a personal speaker manager or a service such as Steve's can spell the difference between speaking success and speaking mediocrity.

The Spirit of NSA

A useful organization for speakers is the National Speaker Association, better known as NSA. This vibrant, collegial professional association has been around since 1973 and has been praised by countless speakers. They feel that NSA was instrumental in their development as skillful speakers and as smart speaking business people. NSA offers such resources as:

1. Thirty-five chapters in the United States where anyone, member or not, can come to hear top speakers sharing their knowledge and experience on relevant speaking topics

2. A fine monthly called *Speaker Magazine,* which runs outstanding articles and columns on all aspects of how to become a successful speaker

3. Friendly and helpful speaking veterans who are always ready and willing to meet with neophyte colleagues and share their advice

4. National and regional events for those who want to drill down deeper into speaking issues and obtain genuinely useful answers from those who have been there

5. A website that includes such tabs as "Speaker Directory," "Learning Experiences" (mainly upcoming events), and "Resources"

6. One day each year designated as *Spirit of NSA Day.* This last item is explained in detail on the NSA website:

> Many members already know, or have heard of, NSA Founder Cavett Robert, CSP, CPAE. He believed the strength of and growth of our profession would prevail if all of our members focus on unconditionally giving of themselves to our community on this day. The NSA community is known for the concept of removing

competition by building a bigger market for all speakers. The strength of NSA is in the education we provide and the strong community we have built. As a member, you are asked to support the Spirit of NSA by introducing colleagues to clients, referring business, or mentoring emerging speakers.

Help the legacy continue and build a bigger NSA pie by participating in Spirit of NSA Day! How you can participate: Provide peer-to-peer encouragement; introduce a colleague to a potential client; refer business to a colleague; mentor an emerging speaker.

In the spirit of Spirit of NSA Day, I must report to you that whenever I have attended an NSA event (I'm a full-fledged, dues-paying member), I've come away with new ideas or new ways of looking at old ideas. The camaraderie of NSA often lends itself to sharing helpful, practical experiences, leads to speaking gigs, the names of event planners, novel techniques for keeping an audience's attention, and other resources such as video producers, book editors, or speaking coaches.

SpeakerNet News

A very useful service to which I subscribe and frequently listen is SpeakerNet News (SNN), run by Rebecca Morgan and Ken Braly since 1996. Committed to serving as a "weekly resource for the speaking, training, and consulting communities," SNN produces and distributes one-hour teleseminar audio interviews with speaking experts on virtually every public speaker item of interest imaginable, at a very reasonable cost.

Many of the quotes in this book came my way from listening to SpeakerNet News interviews. Topics include getting started in the speaking business, sales and marketing, running a business, creating memorable presentations, creating products, and technology. Some of SNN's best-selling teleseminars include "Getting Big-Fee Speaking Engagements from Sponsors, with Vickie Sullivan," "Selling to the Corporate Market: The Who, What and How of It, with Mitchell Goozé, CSP," "The Anatomy of a Remarkable, Convention-Maker Keynote, with Joe Calloway, CSP, CPA," "How to Get on Oprah and Other Talk Shows, with Laurie Fried," and "How to Get Booked and Make Money Forever, with Larry Winget, CSP, CPAE."

But SNN doesn't start and end with teleseminars. Its services also include a weekly e-letter, a Q&A section, Submit a Tip, where speakers can offer other speakers best-practice ideas, a list of quality vendors of products and services that SNN has vetted and feels confident recommending, and three-hour, intensive "doses of immediately usable ideas to help [speakers] bring in more business now."

In many ways SNN offers an online community similar to the in-person communities organized by NSA. By utilizing both these people resources you can grant yourself a "scholarship" in speaker-education studies and ramp your speaking business up to speed in a matter of a few short months. Get the free weekly ezine of best practice tips at www.speakernetnews.com.

Other People Resources

In addition to the people resources I outlined above, there are others I can heartily endorse. Some I've come to know personally, while others have been recommended by people I respect. Here's the list (which will be updated regularly on my website, www.thoughtleading.com/speaking):

Suzanne Bates

Speak Like a CEO Boot Camp with Suzanne Bates is an exceptional executive presentation-skills seminar for leaders "looking to move beyond basic skills so they shine in high-stakes situations." You won't learn this program's tools and techniques anywhere else because they're based on Suzanne's best-selling book *Speak Like a CEO: Secrets to Commanding Attention and Getting Results* (McGraw Hill). Suzanne is the founder and CEO of Bates, a coaching and mentoring firm specializing in helping companies develop their leaders' executive presence and influence. Suzanne is a globally known speaker and thoughtleader.

Check out this seminar and other Bates services at http://www.bates-communications.com/what-we-do/workshops-training/boot-camps.

Alan Weiss

Alan Weiss, CSP, is an inductee into the Professional Speaking Hall of Fame and a recipient of the National Speakers Association Council of Peers Award of Excellence, representing the top 1 percent of professional speakers in the world. He has been named a Fellow of the Institute of Management Consultants, one of only two people in history holding both those designations.

Author of 60 books, his services for speakers include coaching, mentoring, publishing, retreats and seminars (in exotic locations around the globe), his renowned Million Dollar Consulting College, forums, the newsletter Unique Offerings, and much more.

Check it all out at http://www.alanweiss.com/.

Markman Speaker Management

A fee-based placement service specializing in obtaining speaking engagements for clients worldwide, MSM's motto is simple and straight to the point: Get Noticed . . . Get Recognized . . . Get Remembered!

Check out MSM's website at at http://www.markmanspeaker.com/.

Vickie Sullivan

Vickie Sullivan is known worldwide as being the foremost expert on generating revenue for high-end experts. Since 1987 she's worked with thousands of experts in a wide variety of industries to launch their big-fee speaking, professional service, and book/product empires in highly lucrative markets. How does she do it? Through customized solutions created with market analysis and research. Vickie's clients report that her market assessments and intelligence gives them a two-year heads-up on the marketplace.

Check Vickie out at http://www.vickiesullivan.com/.

Darren LaCroix

Darren LaCroix's Stage Time University is for dedicated coaches, authors, pastors, and professional speakers who want to be master presenters. He challenges them with this question: How good could *you* be?

"Presenters waste years of energy and effort trying to figure it out on their own," the Stage Time University Fast Start Membership explains. "[Stage Time] is designed to give you a jump-start on your learning. Save time with insights from over two decades of stage time and learning it the hard way."

Darren is the co-author of the book *Speaker's Edge* (no relation to this book), subtitled *Secrets and Strategies for Connecting with Any Audience* (Soar with Eagles). In 2001 he "outspoke" 25,000 contestants from 14 countries to become Toastmasters' designated "World Champion of Public Speaking."

Check out what Darren has to offer at http://stagetimeuniversity.com/.

David Newman

David Newman, CSP, is a nationally acclaimed marketing speaker known for his high-content, high-energy presentations laced with humor, do-it-now tools, and immediately actionable takeaways. He specializes in working with speakers, authors, consultants, and independent professionals who want to stop throwing money into a marketing black hole and attract, engage, and win more clients.

Author of *Do It! Marketing: 77 Instant-Action Ideas to Boost Sales, Maximize Profits, and Crush Your Competition* (AMACOM

Books), he conducts the Speaker Marketing Workshop, which shows attendees how to identify, precisely target, and get in front of economic buyers who hire paid speakers for associations, conferences, and groups.

Check out his services at http://www.doitmarketing.com/.

Andy Saks

"Is your team tongue-tied?" asks Andy Saks, Spark Presentations, and author of *The Presentation Playbook* (Spark). If so, help them build and deliver a clear, consistent, compelling pitch with presentation skills training, he says. Or arrange for his "speaking anxiety seminars" to be brought into your company.

Andy's firm ensures that trade show booths, sales pitches, and special events are more effective and enjoyable "by training your team to give great presentations" . . . or presenting for you himself when you'd rather use a ringer!

Check out his offerings at http://www.sparkpresentations.com/.

Tom Kennedy

Tom Kennedy and his associates at the The Kennedy Group "help executives develop their message and speak so they will be believed and remembered." Tom's firm teaches skills and strategies for "effective, professional, and memorable communications."

Check it out at http://www.kennedygroupboston.com/index.htm.

TED Talks

TED's website identifies TED Talks as "a nonprofit devoted to spreading ideas, usually in the form of short, powerful talks (18 minutes or less)." Founded in 1984 as a conference where Technology, Entertainment, and Design (TED) converged, TED talks today cover almost all topics, from science to business to global issues, and in more than 100 languages. Independently run TEDx events, TED explains, "help share ideas in communities around the world." There's a speaker participation form to fill out on the website.

Check out that form at https://www.ted.com/participate/nominate.

Toastmasters

Toastmasters International is a world leader in communication and leadership development. Its membership numbers more than 332,000. People join to improve their speaking and leadership skills by attending one of the 15,400 clubs in 135 countries that make up Toastmasters' global network of meeting locations. Motto: "Every Toastmasters journey begins with a single speech."

Check out Toastmasters here: https://www.toastmasters.org/.

SPEAKER NOTES

And Don't Forget *Non-Human* Resources

What about non-human resources, i.e., things? Here are a few of those I can recommend. Again, check my website www.thoughtleading.com/speaking from time to time for an update:

According to Andy Saks, the Earprompter is a "godsend for speakers," allowing us to deliver a presentation word-for-word. On its website, the Earprompter calls itself a technique akin to "The Actor's Secret." It eliminates memorizing, fear, notes, and wasting time. Check it out at http://www.earprompter.com/.

Karen Friedman asks, "Are you looking for an easy-to-use, technology-based tool that will help you and your employees create powerful, effective business presentations?" If so, check out her newly developed Presenter's Pal. Available in both iPad and Android versions, it's designed to "take the stress out of putting together professional presentations." Check it out at http://presenterspal.com/.

Finally, Cardsmith is a cloud-based, tailorable, productivity tool, based on the concept of sticky notes. This innovative resource helps speakers, authors, consultants, and entrepreneurs manage their sales pipeline, marketing initiatives, client engagements, and thought leadership projects. Check it out at http://Cardsmith.co/consulting.

CHAPTER ELEVEN

Negotiating Great Deals

The discussion should never be about fee, only value.

> — ALAN WEISS, PhD, author of *Million Dollar Speaking* (McGraw-Hill)

I F YOU RECALL MY STORY IN CHAPTER TWO about the pro bono diversity conference gig I did in DC that led to a paid diversity conference gig only one month later, here's the follow-up.

On the way back to Boston after the paid gig, I was still marveling over the fact that I ended up in a field of nine speakers at Gallaudet University, all of whom were much more experienced than I in speaking about diversity. So the next day I called the conference planning chief and asked him how I did.

"Very well," he said, "your evaluations all came back very good."

I couldn't help but ask, "I was wondering how I stacked up compared to the other speakers in terms of my fee? You had two keynoters that day in addition to a half dozen very knowledgeable breakout speakers like me. Those speakers all seemed to have a strong grounding in this topic. How much was I paid in relation to them?"

The chief looked over his records, then answered, "You came in #2 in terms of highest paid."

Number 2? I couldn't believe what I just heard. Number 2? "How could that possibly be?" I thought. Then I said it out loud to the conference planner.

"Well, some of the speakers only got a fraction of what you were paid. A few even got no fee at all."

Again I couldn't fathom what I was being told. "How is that?" I asked. "Why would some of those diversity experts get paid so much less than me, or even nothing at all? What did I do differently to earn the fee I did?"

The planning chief chuckled mildly at that, sure of the answer. "Well, it's simple," he said. "You came in #2 in terms of payment for one reason and one reason only . . . you asked for it! A few of the speakers that day got much less than you because that's what they asked for. A couple even volunteered to do it for nothing. One of our two keynoters quoted us a fee that was less than the one you requested.

"You got the fee that you got . . . because you asked for it!"

Fees and Fallbacks

As with publishing articles, when you begin the process of getting speaking engagements, fees should be the farthest thing from your mind. The value of those early gigs is to spread the good word about you to prospects, influencers, colleagues, and anyone else who might pass your name around. To get this experience and exposure, pro bono speaking will be a regular format for you.

However, it doesn't hurt to have a dollar value in your head right from the start, even if you're more than willing to reduce or waive this amount. Whenever someone invites you to speak to a group, you should ask (1) what will be the profile of the attendees? (2) what specific learning objectives or takeaways are needed, and (3) does the group have a budget to work with?

If the answer to the third question is yes, we do have a budget, then make sure that you understand the answer to the second question. Quote the planner whatever fee you might normally charge for such a program, perhaps $5,000 (or whatever you're comfortable with), plus expenses. Then wait to see if he or she blinks. You might get lucky and the planner will say, "Sure, we could afford that." If so, answer calmly, "That will be acceptable." Then draw up an agreement for them to sign, listing all the particulars, and go nuts after you hang up the phone.

More frequently, though, the response is likely to be, "Well, that might be a little steep for us" or "Ah, well, we don't actually have a budget for speaker fees."

If the response to (1) indicates that the audience will clearly be a good one for you, then find a way to do the gig anyway. But don't just lower your fee, because that will suggest that you weren't that valuable in the first place. Instead say, "Well, it sounds like a good group you have there, and I could offer you my program at a lesser fee if we agree on other ways of compensation to make up for the discount." You might then go through some suggested fallback items (see list below).

If the event planner insists they have no budget whatsoever, you might comment that you do conduct a few pro bono talks every year and would be happy to speak without a fee. "But I would appreciate it if you can cover my expenses and I can bring along my assistant (or wife or business partner) at no charge," you might add. Somehow make the group give you *something* in return. That way it will be a true and fair exchange, as it should be, not just a giveaway.

Suggested counter-offer, fallback options might include:

1. An upgraded hotel room if they're at least willing to pay expenses

2. First-class airfare instead of coach

3. Travel expenses paid for two, so that your spouse, friend, assistant, or business partner can travel with you

4. Bulk purchase of your book for everyone in attendance

5. A second hotel night so you can spend some time sightseeing

6. An introduction to VIPs at the conference who might make good prospects for your business or future speaking gigs

7. A list of names and contact info for everyone in attendance

8. An official thank you and endorsement from the association or company president

9. A complimentary year's membership in the organization sponsoring the conference

10. A shorter presentation if possible, e.g., a half-day seminar or 90-minute presentation instead of an all-day seminar.

The idea is to get *something* in return for your willingness to do this for no fee. Note that options 6, 7, 8, and 9 won't cost the organization much and probably would be given to you just for the asking even if you were earning top dollar for this gig. If you can get at least these low-cost items, then even if the event planner refuses your more-costly requests, you won't be giving yourself away for nothing. Never do this, even when starting out.

Negotiating Upward

Then there's the other direction negotiations can take, what I call negotiating upward. Should an event planner say, "That seems high compared to what we've paid our keynoters in the past," you might counter with a value-added suggestion such as, "Well, I'm probably the best at this and so I'm not cheap! But what if I throw in a breakout session in addition to my keynote and write a short article for your newsletter? Would that make my fee more reasonable in your eyes?"

Since you're going to be spending the day at this conference anyway, why not offer your speaking services for a longer period, or to address an additional topic, rather than hang out at the pool or the casino? Offering to do more for your fee might make the difference between having to deal with pressure on you to lower it vs. a quick, even cheerful response like, "OK, sounds good!"

SPEAKER NOTES

Many people ask how to respond when the potential buyer asks, "What's your fee?" The correct answer is, "I don't know, what are your needs?" If you respond to the question with a number, then you admit that you only charge by the time unit. If you respond with a question, then you're telling the customer that fees depend on his or her objectives, and that there are probably options to meet those objectives. Remember: the discussion should never be about fee, only value.

SPEAKER NOTES

Curtis Bingham, Founder and Executive Director of the Chief Customer Officer Council, says, "It might also be worth asking what level of people are in the soliciting organization you're connecting with. Is this a low-level conference producer or the organization's head? If lower level, you might want to try speaking to his or her boss. That way you might be able to have a real negotiation rather than dealing with a middleman."

CHAPTER TWELVE

Delivering Presentations that Knock It Out of the Park

> The best way to find more speaking engagements
> is to deliver a great presentation.
>
> — STEVE HARRISON, publishing, marketing,
> publicity expert, and author of *How to Do*
> *Better Creative Work* (Prentice-Hall Business)

A T THE VERY END OF LARRY WINGET'S TALK on innovative ways to land speaking engagements that I referred to in Chapter Ten, Larry left the stage with a summarizing statement that went something like this: "We can talk about all kinds of creative ways to obtain speaking engagements, but in the end there's one way that will always remain the best tactic of all: just go out and speak. That's the best tactic of all."

Years later, when I did my first, shaky "white guys" diversity presentation, I found that Larry was right. And when I scan the comments from veteran speakers who generously filled out my speaking engagement survey, I notice similar remarks. Doing the best job you can possibly do on a given platform, they agree, may be the single best gig-finding action you can take.

Survey Comments

"Show up and knock it out of the park!"

> — Kathleen Burns Kingsbury, author of *How to Give Financial Advice to Women* and *How to Give Financial Advice to Couples* (both from McGraw-Hill)

"Do a great job on stage. At conferences it gets you additional opportunities such as invitations to do webinars, which lead to additional speeches or work."

> — Suzanne Bates, author of *Speak Like a CEO* and *All the Leader You Can Be* (both from McGraw-Hill)

"Your job on stage is to challenge, stimulate, excite, and motivate, to be the expert. If you want to find the most speaking engagements, you need to do this."

> — Josh Gordon, author of *Presentations that Change Minds: Strategies to Persuade, Convince and Get Results* (McGraw-Hill)

"People see me in action doing my planning consulting work, then ask me to come back for a particular purpose. My favorite speaking story is when a college decided to host a TEDx as a result of my planning work for them, and then asked me to give one of the first talks. That talk has now been seen 25,000 times and counting; it's a major source of credibility for me. And it came about with complete serendipity only because I was there doing work people could see."

— Jay Vogt, author of *Recharge Your Team: The Grounded Visioning Approach* (Praeger Press)

"Someone who attended an event I spoke at unexpectedly contacted a colleague of mine because they did not have my contact info. They had enjoyed the talk and were looking to book me as a keynote."

— Dave Ramsden, author of *Unveiling the Mystic Ciphers: Thomas Anson and the Shepherd's Monument Inscription* (CreateSpace)

SPEAKER NOTES

Steve Harrison: People don't buy speakers. They buy outcomes. So you want to ask your meeting planners, What do you wish your people would do as a result of my speaking? The best way to get speaking engagements is to deliver a great presentation.

Steve Markman: Audiences want to acquire actionable information they can take back to their organizations. They don't want to hear that your firm is the leading firm in this or that subject area. A solid, informative presentation that isn't product- or company-specific will create instant credibility and obviate the need for a sales pitch. A presentation that turns out to be a sales pitch for a product or service will ensure low evaluations by the audience and a one-way ticket home from the conference organizer. The speaker who gives a sales pitch is duly noted and rarely invited back, oftentimes tainting the entire company in the eyes of the event organizer.

Fred Green: Don't rely on PowerPoint either. Just talk to us.

How to Knock It Out of the Park

One magic key to landing more and more speaking engagements is, as Kathleen Burns Kingsbury put it, to "knock it out of the park." If you're doing this consistently, you may not need to read this chapter any further. But if you're someone who consistently knocks it out of the park, you probably will read further because that's the kind of person you are, i.e., always curious about how to do better or about how others succeed, so that you can try something new that might work for you too.

We discussed two tactics in Chapter Nine that apply here: practice your routines in environments where you have little or nothing to lose (speaking before job groups) and where you'll be facing the challenge of grabbing and holding a tough audience's attention (speaking at Rotary club meetings). Lots and lots of experience of this kind will, over years, strengthen your platform skills and season you to become the speaking equivalent of a homerun hitter.

But a helpful prerequisite for becoming a homerun hitter might be to understand the psychology of the event planner. David Newman says that you've got to "keep in mind that meeting planners are lazy, busy, and befuddled," meaning that they're not always sure how to attain the event's true objectives. Josh Gordon puts it this way: "People who hire speakers don't actually care if you are a good speaker or not, or even what your topic is. They just want to put people in their chairs!"

Josh, who has spoken at many high-level conferences in the media and advertising industries, observes that "in every meeting there's always something people need to know about, so if you can talk about that in an interesting way, you can get yourself a speaking engagement." If you can talk about change, for example, as in "how change is affecting an industry as it evolves," you'll have something to say that is insightful." This of course depends on the meeting, he adds, as in what's the ultimate goal of the meeting? Is it to motivate sales people? Help business owners be more successful? Teach attendees investment opportunities?

But when you get down to it, he believes, what a speaker needs to consider beforehand in order to win the speaking engagement is what's going on in that industry now and, in particular, where is that industry heading.

"A lot of associations don't always know about what's going on," he insists, "so go find those people who do, the ones who are really on top of their industry. Call them up and tell them you're planning to do an article about where things are going and that you'd like to interview them for it. Then write your article and use your research as the basis of a speaking proposal."

Josh adds, "You don't have to actually be more of an expert than the experts you interview or who gather at the conference." Your job is not to "out-expert" the experts, your job is to *package* an idea or point of view that gets event attendees motivated, thinking, and discussing."

Josh recalls a non-expert who used to do this repeatedly at conferences serving the broadcast industry. "There was this not-so-smart guy I used to run into who was always talking about 'questions we have to talk about in the coming year.' He had aggregated ten topics he could outline at these events, and it used to amuse me because everyone would always comment that this fellow was 'so on target.' Yet all he had done was aggregate and package what everyone was already talking about! And as a result he created so much interest that conference organizers were always saying, 'Man, we have to get that guy back next year!'"

A publisher Josh knew used to do the same thing, even though he could tell that this publisher didn't seem to know "anything about anything." But the publisher typically would throw out one question at industry meetings to get everyone riled up: "What about the telcoes?" This always caused a rage of conversation at every table, even as Josh realized the publisher had no depth of knowledge of his own, nor any discernible opinion about it.

"Fast forward to a big annual conference," Josh recalls "where this guy got up again and shouted, 'What about those telcoes?' Again, boisterous enthusiasm and energy, an explosion of very controversial dialogue."

What about the telcoes indeed!

CHAPTER THIRTEEN

Maximizing Your Engagements

Expect the best. Capitalize on what comes.

> — Zig Ziglar, legendary motivational
> speaker, salesman, and author of 25 books

In Chapter Four I wrote about the importance of building a followship, particularly building up a robust e-list and then actively using it to stay in constant touch with all your contacts. While I like to make the case that this is the most effective tactic you can use as a follow-up to your presentations, I do recognize that it's not the only one.

The key to speaking success is to not only show up for your speaking gig and knock it out of the park but to also do whatever you can to maximize the engagement so that it positively impacts your followship – so that it adds to your number of followers as well as to the level of loyalty instilled in each of them. Doing little or nothing to maximize your new follower relationships is a missed opportunity of epic proportions!

Here are some more comments from my speaking engagement survey that describe a few of the techniques that speakers use to maximize their speaking engagements, ultimately leading to many more gigs:

Mike Carpenter: I'll usually like to schedule my presentations before a break, during lunch, or at the end of day, and offer to talk with anyone who'd like to talk further at the back of the room during the break directly after my talk. I'll also have a newsletter sign-up sheet available where attendees can leave their name and email address for me to include them in future newsletters I create. Plus I'll include a copy of my book flyer in the presentation handouts.
If the event sponsor allows it, I'll also offer a follow-up conference call or webinar a few days after the presentation for folks who'd like to talk further, as well as include my email address, phone number, and book info and purchase link on all handouts.

Andy Lipman: I ask for testimonials from my audience and then post them on my website.

Kay Keenan: For my topic "How to Write a Marketing Plan in Three Hours Workshop," I offer to review their marketing plan for free. Meeting planners are always impressed.

Louise A. Korver: I provide my email, my links to social media, and will make LinkedIn requests for specific audience members whom I met personally.

Karen Friedman: I post my session review notes and a PDF of my slides for participants to view and download. I also customize a post-session review. They are also subscribed to my video blog and published articles.

Ruby Newell-Legner, CSP: I distribute an evaluation/feedback form in every session that I present. I "bribe" the audience to complete the forms by offering a hearty bonus handout. Using such a system, you can build a database of those who'll want to hire you now or some day in the future.

On the form there are boxes that can be checked if they're interested in receiving a call to discuss training for their group. If they chack the box, I call them. It's that simple.

The key is to reference a tool or checklist during the session, share some of the elements of the document with the group, and if it's robust enough audience members will ask for a copy. When they do I tell them that when they complete the evaluation form and turn it in, I'll make sure that they get a copy.

Pam Harper: I do in-person meetings or phone calls shortly after a gig, then three months later, then one year later. Also, I periodically send relevant articles, podcasts, etc. to my attendees.

Jerry Fletcher: What I do depends on my agreement with the event planner. Things I've done include:

1. Sending PDFs of meeting materials
2. Conducting follow-up webinars on aspects of what I introduced at the event
3. Teleconferences on topics related to the event's core subject
4. One-on-one consulting or coaching with selected individuals (usually at the individual's expense)

Jim Pouliopoulos: When I was a full-time business coach, I would offer a free, one-hour coaching session for anyone who had attended one of my speaking gigs. That tactic sometimes resulted in booking new clients for my coaching program after the sample coaching session.

Allan Lowe: I provide a report via email to all participants after the gig.

Ramsey Bahrawy: I invite my contacts and connections to take a look at my YouTube videos and let me know if they're interested in having me make similar presentations.

Jennifer von Briesen: I try to get business cards or a list of participants for further connections, often offering the full presentation or additional info to those who drop off their cards at the end of my talk.

Jay Vogt: I ask folks to sign up to receive electronic materials of value. I then share the materials and add them to my list. Feels fair.

Kathleen Burns Kingsbury: I'm open to feedback and always ask how can I help more? I am fortunate as my books and my work have built a word-of-mouth-referral system. I do consistent social media, blogs, and published articles, which I am sure contributes as well.

Katy Tynan: I add attendees to my email list, invite them to follow me on social media, and I bring copies of my books to the gig.

Andy Saks: When allowed by the client, I use a survey form that solicits feedback and suggestions on the program, asks them about the ways in which they use presentations and public speaking, then gives them a place to indicate if they're interested in any services I offer and whether/how they'd like to be contacted. I have a paper and online version of this survey and use whichever is appropriate for that audience.

I also tell every audience that I'm at their service and that they're welcome to contact me anytime for advice, suggestions, etc. on the topic I've spoken on. It's a genuine offer and I think they appreciate it.

Warren Greshes, CPAE: I say at end the of my talk, "My business is based on referrals, so if you can help me out with that, I'd appreciate it." Then I follow up every talk with calling or contacting my sponsor afterward, putting a bug in their ear by saying, "Y'know I could also speak on X and Y for you in the future" and "I'd love to get any contact referrals you could give me."

Hugh Culver: I ask for referrals by putting a pile of eight referral forms face down on an eight-seat table. These are papers where they can also get invited to my free webinar and can check a box if they want to bring me in to their upcoming conference or other event.

Keith Long: I put a call-to-action element into my speech.

Parmelee Eastman: I get their business cards, I note their questions on the back, and then I follow up with each individually. I also write up notes of my talk and send them out to all attendees. I ask, too, to link up with me on LinkedIn.

Jerry Vieira: I always call those who came up to me after the talk and gave me their cards, asking me to follow up with them. Typically those are the folks who lead to consulting engagements.

Gina Abudi: I make available my white papers, my book, my topic slide templates and tools, and other downloads.

On the Other Hand!

What about the flip side? What mistakes do speakers make that will ensure that they never get asked back again by the event planner? Or that their target audiences leave feeling like they didn't get their money's worth?

Here are a few thoughts on this from event planners and from speakers who have sponsored other speakers from time to time . . . and have learned decisively what *not* to do:

Louise A. Korver: Some speakers want a particular type of yogurt on ice on the podium or they want a green room all their own, or a special type of transportation (first-class airfare, Uber to and from the airport, etc.). Don't be high maintenance.

Pam and Scott Harper: We are turned off by speakers who are disrespectful of us, especially those who don't bother to get us materials (photos, bios, blurbs) in a timely manner. Also, by speakers who show up late on the day of the event!

Kathleen Burns Kingsbury: Not communicating. Being demanding or derogatory to staff. If you want to get hired again, be easy and pleasant to work with and treat everyone from the CEO to the tech guy respectfully.

Gina Abudi: When they act like prima donnas!

Fred Green: Don't self-promote on stage! I call that the kiss of death. Don't start talking about your company and what you can do for everyone and what your fees are, etc. Just deliver your presentation. There's no better way to turn off an audience than to say "Buy my product!"

Jennifer von Briesen: Some speakers don't seem to know much or care much about our organization or building a partnership/relationship. Others agree to come and speak, then bail at the last minute due to other work conflicts (really disappointing). I don't like how some speakers waltz in and do their talk, then leave immediately without staying a few moments to chat and answer follow-up questions.

Keith Long: Not being responsive to the audience.

Harold Schroeder, FCMC, PMP, CHRL, CHE: I make sure I get business cards and/or contact information from all I meet and then send everyone a follow-up email.

Parmelee Eastman: Speakers who just sell themselves instead of providing useful information to the audience.

Jerry Fletcher: Prima donnas I can do without. That and not returning calls or emails in a reasonable time frame.

Norman Daoust: Not managing the clock, i.e., running overtime.

Mike Carpenter: Speakers who don't show up early to introduce themselves to the event manager. Or they leave the event immediately after their presentation. Also some speakers are poorly prepared and/or attempt to cover too much material. These speakers often leave no time for a Q&A or discussion after the formal presentation.

CHAPTER FOURTEEN

Finding Your Path to Speaking Success

You are the master of your destiny.

> — Napoleon Hill, author of *Think and Grow Rich*

WHILE I WAS WORKING ON THIS BOOK, a friend from a professional consultants organization contacted me with an invitation to speak to her group's members about the topic of landing speaking gigs. I chuckled at that because it reminded me (a) how important writing a book is in that it lends the kind of credibility that can lead to a speaking gig and (b) that gigs can come your way via any number of avenues, even when a speaker is in the *process* of writing a book as opposed to having completed one. Say it again with me: Ya just never know.

In my speaking engagement survey, speakers reported other examples of gigs coming about in unusual or outright weird ways:

Katy Tynan: Via Twitter, as a direct message.

Karen Friedman: Someone found me on LinkedIn and invited me to run a two-day program with hospital executives in China. I went. It was awesome.

Pam Harper: I once cold-called CEOs who weren't able to attend an event I had self-sponsored and offered to privately present highlights. I had one taker out of 100 calls. Following up on the private presentation, I periodically stayed in touch. One year later the CEO asked me to lead an executive offsite.

Keith Long: I was shopping and struck up a conversation with a stranger.

Ramsey Bahrawy: A local senior center asked me to speak on the Spring Revolution in the Middle East.

Jerry Fletcher: Conversation across the aisle on an airplane.

Glen Earl: Speaker called in sick so sponsoring company called me one day before the keynote.

Kay Keenan: As a result of me being a volunteer organizer of Wilmington Garden Day, I had to recruit others to help staff a garden. A woman I vaguely knew from church asked me about my signature block "Author of Conversation on Networking: How to build relationships for life" as she was in a group where they were looking for speakers. From this encounter, I can now count more than ten speaking engagements that followed.

Mike Carpenter: An out-of-the-blue referral from a networking contact to help him with a two-day-long professional development program for the top 40 sales people of a global Fortune 100 firm, which has little to do with the industry I normally focus on.

Parmelee Eastman: A request out of the blue to speak in India.

Jerry Vieira: Through an article posted online that arose from an IMC talk.

Suzanne Bates: Though I can't think of any weird ones, what I *will* say is that you never know when a good speech five years ago will be remembered and prompt people to pick up the phone. You never know when someone who saw you speak years ago will be on a committee looking for speakers for a conference and recommend you. In other words, if you are relevant and memorable, when opportunity arises, you will be top of mind.

So sometimes speaking will just come to you if you only sit there, or ride on an airplane, or push a shopping cart, or log onto social media. But even then, you probably planted a seed somehow, whether in the past or at that very moment. Speaking gigs do abound and you'll find them if you try, or they'll find you. Perhaps a technique in this book will help, or perhaps one will just come out of the blue. But they are findable.

You can plant, grow, succeed, and enjoy. That's the mantra to keep in mind. Plant, grow, succeed, enjoy. Four little words, four notions, four aspirations and guideposts.

Recite them to yourself while you notice more and more speaking engagements hurtling your way, coming now fast and furious in your direction like they've never come before.

After all, it's all about trying things, believing great things can happen, and then refusing to give up. That's your path to speaking success, your roadmap and GPS for getting there.

It's your speaker's edge.

INDEX

ABOUT THE AUTHOR

CHIEF IMAGINATIVE OFFICER (CIO) of emerson consulting group, Ken Lizotte CMC is also author of *The Expert's Edge: Become the Go-To Authority that People Turn to Every Time* (McGraw-Hill) and six other books as well as 600+ published articles. Since 1996, his firm has guided over 350 experts and professional service firms to achieve the elite status of *published thoughtleader* by providing services that ensure the publication of their  articles and books. Emerson consulting group also offers speaking engagement placement, book promotion programs, social media campaigns, and traditional publicity services.

A popular speaker himself, Ken has addressed such target audiences as the American Management Association, the Institute of Management Consultants, the National Speakers Association, the CEO Club of Boston, and Harvard University. He has been interviewed by *Fortune Magazine*, the *New York Times*, *Fast Company*, *Business Week*, *Newsweek*, *Investors Business Daily*, *Writer's Digest*, CBS-TV and National Public Radio.

Ken resides with his family in Concord, Massachusetts, and is president of the board of directors at Thoreau Farm, the birthplace of Henry David Thoreau.

Note: To learn more about Ken's services and the speakers quoted in this book as well as stay up-to-date on speaking trends, resources, customized advice, and other topics in the preceding pages, visit www.thoughtleading.com/speaking.